SHORT CUTS

INTRODUCTIONS TO FILM STUDIES

T0312575

OTHER SELECT TITLES IN THE SHORT CUTS SERIES

BIO-PICS

A LIFE IN PICTURES

ELLEN CHESHIRE

WALLFLOWER

LONDON and NEW YORK

A Wallflower Press Book

Wallflower Press is an imprint of
Columbia University Press
Publishers Since 1893
New York, Chichester, West Sussex
cup.columbia.edu

Cover image: *Lincoln* (2012) © Dreamworks/20th Century Fox

A complete CIP record is available from the Library of Congress

ISBN 978-0-231-17205-9 (pbk. : alk. paper)
ISBN 978-0-231-85068-1 (e-book)

Columbia University Press books are printed on permanent and durable acid-free paper.
This book is printed on paper with recycled content.

Printed in the United States of America

p 10 9 8 7 6 5 4 3 2 1

CONTENTS

This book is dedicated to all my friends and family
who have to hear me say 'It's Bio-Pics as in Biographical Pictures
(films about real people), not Bi-opics, which sounds like some
kind of sight problem'

'The one duty we owe history is to re-write it.'
– Oscar Wilde, *The Critic as Artist* (1891)

INTRODUCTION: A LIFE IN PICTURES

> Definition: Bio-pic aka Biographical Picture — a film that depicts the life of a real person, past or present.

> Studios have looked to the ever-increasing obsession with celebrity and justifiably assumed it translates to, if not guaranteed success then at the very least a big head start. They have some great figures to back that up too.
> — Giles Hardie, *Sydney Morning Herald* (25 October 2013)

A quick survey of one week's film stories for the national UK newspaper *The Guardian* (26 August–1 September 2014) revealed six bio-pic related features: a review of the bio-pic on Italian poet Giacomo Leopardi which opened at the Venice Film Festival; rumours that Martin Scorsese is to make a film about the Ramones; news and clips on the new Jimi Hendrix bio-pic, *Jimi: All Is by My Side*; an interview with actor John Hamm on sporting bio-pic *Million Dollar Arm*; a news story on a court case surrounding the 2013 Linda Lovelace bio-pic and news on Lifetime TV's forthcoming *The Brittany Murphy Story*.

As the *Economist* stated:

> It's that time of year again — the time when the Oscars and the BAFTAs are within sniffing distance, and every major studio releases the prestige pictures which may just snag a few awards. Inevitably,

several of those films are biopics. Oscar voters love them because the 'based on a true story' tag gives them a veneer of seriousness, and because it's easy to judge whether or not the central impersonation is any good. (NB 2011)

The 2014 award season featuring films from 2013/14 was once again a who's who of screen who's whos: *12 Years a Slave, Dallas Buyers Club, Philomena, The Wolf of Wall Street, Behind the Candelabra, Captain Phillips, American Hustle, Saving Mr Banks, The Butler, The Invisible Woman, Mandela: Long Walk to Freedom, Rush* and *Good Vibrations* were all nominated in major categories at the BAFTAs and/or Academy Awards. At both ceremonies, all five Best Supporting Actors were nominated for playing real people. Barkhad Abdi in *Captain Phillips,* Bradley Cooper in *American Hustle,* Michael Fassbender in *12 Years a Slave,* Jonah Hill in *The Wolf of Wall Street* and Jared Leto in *Dallas Buyers Club.*

Despite the incredible popularity of the bio-pic both at the box office and at award ceremonies, surprisingly there has been very little critical writing on them – just two books. The first, George F. Custen's *Bio/Pics: How Hollywood Constructed Public History* (1992) focuses on films produced in Hollywood from the 1930s to the 1960s. In his introduction he declared that at the time he was writing, in 1991, the genre was in decline:

> The biopic seems since the 1960s to have faded away to a minor form. Today, it is seen most frequently on cable channels, in rare contemporary form like *The Doors* (1991) or *Sweet Dreams* (1985), or in intriguing transmutations of made-for-TV movies. (1992: 2)

The second, Dennis Bingham's *Whose Lives Are They Anyway: The Biopic as Contemporary Film Genre* (2010), focuses on the 'evolution and life-cycle changes of the genre'. He also sees biographies of men and women as essentially different genres:

> Films about men have gone from celebratory to warts-and-all to investigatory to post-modern to parodic. Biopics of women, on the other hand, are weighed down by myths of suffering, victimization, and failure perpetuated by a culture whose films reveal an acute fear of women in the public realm. (2010: 10)

Bingham's book, split into two sections – 'The Great (White) Man Biopic and its Discontents' and 'A Woman's Life is Never Done: Female Biopics' – examines predominantly American films from the 1930s to the 2000s, through these gender distinctions.

A few more years and Custen would have seen a slow re-awakening of the bio-pic that, by the mid-1990s and into the twenty-first century, has increasingly become a staple of both Hollywood and commercial world cinema. This period closely mirrors that of a wider societal fascination with the private lives of stars through magazines such as *Hello!* and *Heat*, and television format mutations such as *Dancing with the Stars*, *Dancing on Ice*, *Celebrity Apprentice*, *I'm a Celebrity... Get Me Out of Here!* and talent show format series.

This fascination is not new. There has always been a keen interest in the private lives of celebrities. In the 1740s the artist William Hogarth produced a print comparing the height of the leading stage actor of the day, David Garrick, with those of his contemporaries – it was a best seller. When the Victorian stage actor Sir Henry Irving (most popularly known now as the inspiration for Bram Stoker's *Dracula*), arrived for the American leg of his World Tour in 1896 journalists rowed out to his ship, to be the first to interview this titan of the British stage, and on landing he was carried aloft amongst thousands of well-wishers who had never seen him before – they were transfixed by the draw of fame.

Representations of famous lives were a popular theatrical staple long before the arrival of cinema. William Shakespeare's historical output, which includes *Julius Cesar*, *Henry IV*, *Henry V*, *Richard III* and *Anthony and Cleopatra*, did not let the facts get in the way of a good story. *Ian Hislop's Olden Days* (BBC, 2014), explores our fascination with the past, focusing on great figures from British history. In the first episode Hislop's opening gambit is that, 'the Olden Days have the best characters, and the best stories – but not necessarily the best facts'. This notion of playing fast and loose with historical facts is one that seems to trouble both film critics and historians, and will be explored in this volume.

Although the films themselves frequently get a critical drubbing, their success at the box office and on the award circuit for the past two decades demands a further examination of this much maligned and misunderstood genre. But is the bio-pic in fact a genre in its own right? Or are the films merely footnotes in other more traditional genres such as the western, the musical, the war movie or the costume drama depending on the historical figure under scrutiny? Unlike other genre forms the bio-pic seemingly shares no familiar iconography, codes or conventions. They can be set anywhere and at any time. What links them is quite simply the films depict the life of an important real person. Clearly Bingham believes that: 'The biopic is a genuine, dynamic genre and an important one. The biopic narrates, exhibits, and celebrates the life of a subject in order to demonstrate, investigate, or question his or her importance in the world' (2010: 10).

Yet, in 'Big names, big flops: Why the biopics have failed in 2013', Giles Hardie's running theme is that bio-pics are not a genre:

> Biopics can work and be utterly brilliant, if they are also great thrill-ers (*Rush, The Impossible, Captain Phillips*), epics (*Young Victoria*), political dramas (*The Queen*), tragedies (*Milk, The Pianist*) or tales of triumph and redemption (*Erin Brockovich, The Railway Man*). They can't work if their makers don't choose a genuine storytell-ing genre that makes their mark on the reality. Biography is the shelf you might find the book on, but it isn't itself a narrative style. (2013)

This volume offers-up a series of case studies that will throw light on this complex genre, analysing them in terms of their similarities – characters, plots, themes and motifs – and points of difference – structure and intent. Each film considered will thus assist in this exploration of the following questions posed:

1. Why is the genre enjoying such a resurgence?
2. Who are suitable candidates for bio-pic treatment?
3. How much of a life has to be included for a film to be a bio-pic and how are their stories told?
4. How have the issues surrounding the subject's representa-tion/misrepresentation contributed to the genre?
5. Does the choice of actor and their approach to the role affect this representation?
6. What response do these films have critically and commer-cially?

The structure of the book is based on the kind of study I was searching for when I first started teaching bio-pics as part of a course on film genres. I wanted a book where the films were central and would help to stimulate discussion on key concerns and responses to the genre. I have therefore grouped contrasting films based around similar professions or sub-genres: musicians, actors/directors, writers, artists, sportsmen, academics, politicians and royalty which allows for comparisons to be drawn in approaches to similar milieu, professional characteristics and backgrounds.

Bio-pics have been and seemed destined to remain so prevalent that this study can only offer an analysis of a small percentage of films that have been produced. I have had to make tough decisions, and have selected not necessarily the 'greatest' examples, but certainly popular ones that contribute to the debate. All the films are in English, released since 1994, and are widely available on DVD. I have added a further viewing section at the end of each grouping.

Defining a bio-pic is notoriously difficult; unlike most other genres there is no specific set of codes or conventions. For the purposes of this book, some guidelines and parameters have had to be set in order to begin the process of shaping genre expectations and conventions. I have had to dismiss films that are 'Inspired by...' such as *Mrs Brown* (1997) or *The Terminal* (2004). Admittedly, the inspiration for the narrative may be a real person, but the filmmakers have taken facts that are known and woven a fictional tale around them, so they have been eliminated from this study.

So have films where the plot revolves around a completely fabricated premise, such as the actor hired to play the first screen-version of Dracula, Max Schreck, really being a vampire (*Shadow of a Vampire,* 2000); how was it that a servant girl painted by Johannes Vermeer was wearing an expensive pearl earring (*The Girl with a Pearl Earring,* 2003) or a version of history where Christian Slater plays Winston Churchill as a young American cigar-chewing war hero in the satire on American war movies *Churchill: The Hollywood Years* (2004)? These may be real names, but the set-ups entirely undocumented or unbelievable.

The last category excluded are the thinly-veiled bio-pics where character names have changed but are considered to be based on a known person such as Eminem (*8 Mile*, 2002), Kurt Cobain (*Last Days*, 2005), Diana Ross and the Supremes (*Dreamgirls*, 2006) and L. Ron Hubbard (*The Master*, 2012).

Scarlett Johansson as Griet and Colin Firth as the Dutch painter Johannes Vermeer in
Girl with a Pearl Earring (2003)

The films being examined in the case studies included here are ones where real names have been used, ones where the filmmakers have made a conscious choice to tell the story of a known person, and where audiences arriving at a cinema would have previous knowledge or expectation of what they are likely to see. If the subject is new to them, they would be able to leave safe in the knowledge that further research could be undertaken to determine the veracity of the film.

1. Why is the genre enjoying such a resurgence?

> It is not hard to see why biopics have become a cinema staple. The genre has obvious appeal for producers and distributors: the stories are ready-made, the subjects are often well known, and the finished product often has, in theory at least, a built-in audience.
> – John Hazelton, *Screen International* (2005)

In an era of mass entertainment with films competing with a whole host of other entertainment forms, cinema has an increasingly commercial imperative. Rather than creating innovative material there has been a tendency to be cautious and produce films which are familiar and safe. Sequels and films based on previous known material such as literary adaptations and bio-pics have become an essential element of this output. According to the *BFI Statistical Yearbook 2013*, of the twenty most successful films at the UK box office in 2012 only two were based on original material.

People may well recognise the subject of the film but not necessarily know how they achieved greatness and/or subsequent disgrace or why they are worthy of being given the bio-pic treatment. Hence a familiar pattern of starting with the subject at their moment of greatness or weakness and then stepping back in time to see how they reached this point. 'If you already know about the person being profiled, you're annoyed by how much is distorted and omitted. If you aren't an expert going into the cinema, you're never sure how much of what you see on screen actually happened in real life' (NB 2011).

If the film is based on a writer, composer, artist, musician, director or actor there are further opportunities for promotion and sales through book tie-ins and reissues of CDs and films. But 'the key thing is that it's not about the awareness levels for the subject. It's about making the subject's life seem extraordinary. If you convince people that it's an extraordinary story that needs to be told, who the person is behind that becomes secondary' (Hazelton 2005).

Therefore, the little-known lives of protagonists such as Erin Brockovich who single-handedly brought down a Californian water company in *Erin Brockovich* (2000) or the Nobel Prize-winning physicist John Nash in *A Beautiful Mind* (2001) have been translated into box office and award-winning hits without a great deal of public foreknowledge of their subject. However, they both needed to cast major stars (Julia Roberts and Russell Crowe) to play these unknowns, to help increase box office potential.

2. Who are suitable candidates for bio-pic treatment?

If the greatest friend of the biopic is research, then its greatest enemy is deference. – Barbara Ellen, *The Times* (2002)

The definition at the start of this book implies that the basic tenet of a bio-pic is that it must be based on a real and important person. But that is not such a simple guideline as it first appears.

During the Hollywood Golden Age (approximately 1930–1960) there was a tendency to focus on great historical figures. From Julius Caesar to Joan of Arc, Napoleon to Elizabeth I, many of history's greatest figures have become inextricably bound to their screen images. Over 160 actors have tackled the role of Napoleon (the earliest being in 1897, with the most famous early portrayal being Albert Dieudonne in Abel Gance's six-hour 1926 version right up to the 2001 comedy-drama *Emperor's New Clothes* with Ian Holm). There have been over 120 on-screen Lincolns (most recent: Daniel Day-Lewis, 2012) and numerous Hitlers (most recent: Ian Hart, 2011), Queen Victorias (most recent: Emily Blunt, 2009) and Queen Elizabeth the Firsts (most recent: Cate Blanchett, 2007). If we head to the Wild West, Buffalo Bill, Billy the Kid, Jesse James, Wild Bill Hickock, General Custer and Wyatt Earp are frequent on-screen presences.

In the past twenty years this more historical canon has made occasional appearances whilst a greater dominance has been placed on figures from the twentieth century, with the majority of subjects in recent living memory (in some cases, still alive) who will have that all important awareness and fan-base.

However, it is not just an impressive back-catalogue or headline grabbing notoriety that justifies the bio-pic treatment. Inevitably the cliché of the tortured genius is a popular model, providing us with a pre-written storyline, melodrama and a strong central performance.

A survey of the musicians depicted sees a collection of alcohol and drug addicts prone to violent outbursts and tragic love lives. For the men, the subjects must be seen to battle their demons and be triumphant (of sorts): *Ray* (2004) and *Walk the Line* (2005) both end at a moment of victory. For the women, the films dwell on their victimhood, exploiting their tragedy to a greater degree than their male counterparts as in *Lady Sings the Blues* (1972), *What's Love Got to Do with It?* (1993) and *La Vie en Rose* (2007). The trend continues as Jeff Sneider reports:

> Almost as soon as Whitney Houston died in February 2012, the blogosphere erupted with stories that pondered who could play the famed singer in a biopic, which is considered Hollywood's highest post-mortem tribute. Houston experienced incredible highs and tragic lows during her rollercoaster of a life, which would be ripe for cinematic tribute *à la* the Tina Turner movie *What's Love Got to Do With It?* Angela Bassett and Laurence Fishburne earned Oscar nominations for that film. (2013)

Those with a film actor or director at their heart seem to relish in the frame-by-frame recreation of key scenes from the subject's films. Often actors are lost in an excess of prosthetics, costume, make-up and wigs, period detail and dialect work, that what remains are often poor facsimiles of the original.

The creative process and exploration of writers' work is difficult to achieve cinematically. It is hard to make the act of sitting alone writing in a room visually or emotionally engaging. Hence the act itself is largely ignored in favour of the complex emotional lives of the writers. A similar conundrum is created with the artists' bio-pics. These too, often fail to deal with the art, usually concentrating on the artist's tortured life, but give no sense of how the art was created or of the work itself.

In the sports arena the sport takes centre-stage, even if off-screen. The actor cast has usually had to transform themselves physically for the role (Will Smith in *Ali*, 2001) and this objectification of the their new physique coupled with the built-in tension of the outcome of each match (*The Damned United*, 2009) or race (*Rush*, 2013) creates a series of 'what if' story questions, that may eclipse the emotional elements of the lives.

In its heyday of the 1930s the scientific bio-pic focused on the lives of laboratory research scientists such as Marie Curie (discovered radium), Paul Ehrlich (found the cure for syphilis) and Louis Pasteur (developed vaccines). In more recent years, the tendency has been to look not at figures from the hard sciences but rather on academics whose research field fall within the soft sciences, dealing with social (*Kinsey*, 2004) and psychological (*A Dangerous Method*, 2012) conditions. This allows for the additional presentation of the academics' research through the prism of their psychological or social circumstances.

Just as history has produced some inspiring and less inspiring political leaders, cinema has produced a similarly mixed bag of political bio-pics. These films will inevitably be subject to intense scrutiny; the politics of the screenwriters, directors and actors will be questioned. They will be examined from both sides of the political divide as to whether the film has distorted facts or made script/casting choices to fit some larger political agenda. Accusations will be made that filmmakers have made the politician too caricatured? (*W*, 2008); too likeable? (*The Iron Lady*, 2011); too dull? (*César Chávez*, 2014); too saintly? (*Invictus*, 2009).

From Henry VIII to Princess Diana, there has always been a fascination with filmic representations of the British Royal Family. The first British actor to win an Academy Award won it for a bio-pic: Charles Laughton for *The*

Private Life of Henry VIII (1933) but Naomi Watts did not fare so well for her central performance in *Diana* (2013). The only award she received was the anti-Oscar, the Golden Raspberry. These films tend to be concerned with getting the period details right and are exquisite examples of the work of production and costume designers. As with the political films there will inevitably be cries of 'it didn't happen like that'. What the Royal Family say in their domestic space is a matter pure speculation. Can they be treated as 'real' or as purely 'propaganda'? Or more importantly should they be treated as real or as entertainment?

3. How much of a life has to be included and how are they told

> There is nothing duller on screen than being accurate but undra-matic.
> – Darryl F. Zanuck, Twentieth Century Fox Studio Head, 1933–1971
> (quoted in Whiteclay 1996: 101)

Good advice, but directors of bio-pics often find themselves at the sharp end of criticism when their films are released. With directors challenged for overstating the good or evil of its subject matter or twisting the reality of events for the purpose of film.

> The trouble with conventional biopics is that they invariably fall short in both the 'bio' and the 'pic' departments. That is, they don't have enough narrative momentum to engage as dramas, but they have too much fudging and falsifying to qualify as biographies. (NB 2011)

This is a genre that often gets slated, as concerns are raised that it is the more popular film versions of history that will be the one that people see and remember. When most people come across a photo of General George S. Patton, they expect to see an image of George C. Scott from *Patton* (1970). And they think incorrectly that Captain Bligh as played by Trevor Howard in *Mutiny on the Bounty* (1962) routinely flogged his crew. In *A Man For All Seasons* (1966), Thomas More (Paul Scofield) is presented as a benevolent martyr whereas biographies tell us that this version of More is far from the real person, who demanded the blood of Protestants and gloated when they burned.

Bio-pics share the same fate as literary adaptations: what to leave in or take out and how to create drama out of internal monologues. Screenwriter Stephen J. Rivele [who, with Christopher Wilkinson, wrote *Nixon* and *Ali*] said:

> We do a lot of research before we start. We don't start writing before we have a clear understanding of the nature of the characters and the events that we want to portray, so when we get to those lacunae of research where there is no hard evidence about what was actually said, or how situations were resolved, we make it up. That's what we do as dramatists. We make it up based upon our best understanding of the character, his or her circumstances, and the nature of the relationships in the scene. (Quoted in Coppola 2002: 16)

A problem for the bio-pic is that real life does not always fit the dramatic structure needed for a mainstream movie. A scant chronology akin to a Wikipedia entry can lack momentum and appear as a plodding step-by-step move from birth to death. Merely showing where a subject has come from and how they achieved their success (and then possible decline) does not necessarily create a compelling narrative.

Filmmakers have approached this barrier with varying degrees of success. Some would argue that unless the point is to take a good measure of an entire life, or a good percentage, it is not a bio-pic. With that criteria *Ray* would be in, and *The Motorcycle Diaries* (2004) out.

However, I will argue that we can learn more about a person in a well-constructed/written 'narrative week' if that week, is a significant period in their life such as *The Queen* (2007) than, say, *Creation* (2009) which, despite focusing on Darwin's emotional relationships with his daughter, wife and colleagues, is curiously dispassionate.

The films explored in this volume cover a wide variety of narrative time-frames from the previously mentioned one-week duration of *The Queen* to the near cradle-to-grave structure of *Mandela: Long Walk to Freedom* (2013) which attempts to cover the first sixty years (two-thirds) of Nelson Mandela's life in 140 minutes.

There will be discussions on the films' narrative structures, including those that:

- take a chronological view of a life; often starting at an incredible high or low point within that life and then flash-back to the start to see how that success or failure was reached (for example, *Walk the Line* and *Pollock* (2000))
- take a completely linear beginning-to-end view of a short period of time (for example, *The Queen* and *Lincoln* (2012))
- throw the viewer back and forward in time as events in the present trigger memories of the past (for example, *Ray* and *Iris* (2001))
- create a complex non-linear narrative structure combining historical fact with fantasy that contradicts the expected norms of the traditional bio-pic (for example, *American Splendor* (2003) and *I'm Not There* (2007))

Is it the job of the filmmaker to ensure historical accuracy? Perhaps deviation and omission are permissible when trying to create a compelling film. As Giles Hardie writes, 'you need a better storyteller for biopics than for fiction. The truth is a huge handicap to storytelling: real life doesn't come in three act structures and real people complain about discrepancies between the actual events and those portrayed' (2013).

4. Issues of representation/misrepresentation

> The biopic is a discredited and disreputable genre, because so many bio-pics tell lies about their subjects.
> — Paul Byrnes, *Sydney Morning Herald* (2003)

Here, Byrnes has clearly articulated one of the powerful concerns around the genre: sometimes bio-pics stretch the truth and tell a life story with varying degrees of accuracy. In a period of vigorous legislative concerns and the power of the print media, producers are increasingly concerned over a subject's portrayal. Mark Gill, President of Warner International Pictures, said, 'You need to be very accurate – scrupulously so – unless you want to get smacked. Because if you aren't, somebody is going to do the research and find out you've changed this and this and this, or that the person didn't do that.' He cited *Good Night, and Good Luck* (2005) – amongst other things a portrait of Broadcast journalist Edward R. Murrow – on which he had worked, where screenwriters George Clooney and Grant Heslov looked for two independent sources for each fact (see Hazelton 2005).

Steve Ryfle urged screenwriters to take steps to protect themselves if their project is based on a real person:

> Everyone owns their own life story, and has the right to sell it to the highest bidder. So far, Hollywood has faced only a relatively small number of lawsuits alleging that life stories have been stolen and unaccredited. No longer is it possible for a filmmaker to get away with the disclaimer at the film's beginning or end that the story is 'based on true events, but dramatic license has been taken: people's names have been changed, characters composited, events fabricated or deleted or re-ordered'. (2005)

The practice of suing is certainly not a new phenomenon. In 1933, Hollywood got a shock when Prince Felix Yusupov and Princess Irina Yusupov (the model for the film's Princess Natasha) successfully sued MGM for the way they were represented in *Rasputin and the Empress* (1932). The lawsuit gave rise to the 'all persons fictitious' disclaimer that has since become standard for all fiction films.

Such elaborate opening or closing disclaimers about characters and events being fiction – even when they are clearly based on the lives of real people – will not necessarily protect the filmmakers from a legal onslaught. Therefore, is it wise for a producer to secure the support of the subject (if still alive) and their family and friends prior to the film beginning production? This may aid the production/promotion process but may lead to temptation to offer a hagiography rather than the story that needs to be told to create drama and entertainment. For creative artists whose work is still in copyright, support from the family and/or estate is crucial in obtaining rights to use their work. In John Maybury's *Love is the Devil* (1998) none of Francis Bacon's paintings were shown as the painter's estate refused permission. The film focuses on Bacon's visual obsessions rather than the art. *Jimi: All Is by My Side*, with André Benjamin, aka the rapper André 3000, playing Jimi Hendrix, was made without the permission of the Hendrix estate and as a consequence features none of his music. The film, set in London 1966 – 67 in the run-up to the release of his début album, *Are You Experienced?*, shows Benjamin/Hendrix performing cover versions of period rock classics.

Some family members may initially grant permission to a director, especially when an attractive star name is attached. Such was the case when Tina Sinatra (Frank's daughter), having given permission for Martin Scorsese to film her father's life story, had second thoughts when she learned he wanted to show the 'violent, sexually-charged, hard-drinking Frank', Tina had wanted to show the 'softer side of her dad and let the focus be on the music' (Singh 2009).

The Mandela family and supporters were integral to the making and promotion of *Mandela: Long Walk to Freedom*. The film shows Mandela's life as a rural boy herding cattle in the Eastern Cape, leading up to his inauguration as president of South Africa in 1994. It also depicts the darker aspects of Mandela's family relationships. However, the reverence in which Mandela was held by those involved led to an overly safe and 'uncinematic' film in terms of engaging narratve. The film's producer, David Thompson, said, 'It is a very difficult story to give a dramatic shape to ... We felt such a responsibility to the subject ... We were too much in awe' (quoted in Williams 2013).

Mary Stone could not help but notice that in 2012 two films about her grandfather Alfred Hitchcock had been made: *The Girl* and *Hitchcock*. 'We [the family] just decided a long time ago, you can't stop someone from publishing something or shooting a movie about something. We just take no opinion of the individuals or works because we know the true story. To be honest with you, we completely ignore those kinds of things because they are not true and can be very hurtful to the family' (2013).

Anthony Hopkins as Alfred Hitchcock on the *Psycho* set in *Hitchcock* (2012)

Alfred Hitchcock on the *Psycho* set for cinematic trailer (1960).

In his introduction to *Past Imperfect: History According to the Movies,* Carnes states:

> Like drama and fiction, movies inspire and entertain. They often teach important truths about the human condition. They do not provide a substitute for history, which has been painstakingly assembled from the best available evidence and analysis. But sometimes filmmakers wholly smitten by their creations, proclaim them to be historically 'accurate' or 'truthful', and many viewers presume them to be so. Viewers should neither accept such claims nor dismiss them out of hand, but regard them as an invitation for further exploration. (1996: 9–10)

5. Casting and performance

> The biggest problem facing any conscientious maker of a biographical movie must be the casting. You can fatten them up, give them false noses and shave off their hair, but most film stars remain malleable only to a limited degree ... on the other hand, if the star is so transformed as not be recognisable, where is the attraction for the fan? – Geoff Brown, *The Times* (2004)

The magnitude of the life being rendered does not necessarily equate to a film's success. This could be brought about by an over-familiarity of a subject or their on-screen representation. This is possibly the reason behind disappointing reviews and box office returns for *Ali* starring Will Smith. One would have thought a film about one of America's greatest sporting heroes being played by one the world's most bankable and likeable stars would have been a box office draw. However, this was not the case. Perhaps Ali fans had too recently seen the documentary *When We Were Kings* (1996) with Ali himself to be interested in seeing a facsimile in the shape of Will Smith, and perhaps Will Smith fans were not keen on seeing the smart, charming and witty star being beaten to a pulp and becoming a shadow of the former star, as with the man himself.

In recent years, there have been two examples where within months of each other where two films have been released about the same person, which lend themselves to clear comparisons for analysis. In 2005 and 2006 a double bill of films about Truman Capote – *Capote* and *Infamous*, respectively – were released, with both covering exactly the same time period in his life: the researching and writing of his true crime book *In Cold Blood*. The two films are very different both in performance and tone – inevitably it was the first released (*Capote* starring Philip Seymour Hoffman) which won the critical plaudits, box office receipts and shelves of awards, whilst the second (*Infamous* with Toby Jones), perhaps the superior film, failing to reach such heights.

In 2012 Toby Jones was first to appear on screen as Alfred Hitchcock in a HBO/BBC TV film *The Girl* that centred on the filming of Hitchcock's *The Birds* (1963) and his fascination with Tippi Hedren (played by Sienna Miller). A few months later cinema audiences saw Anthony Hopkins as the eponymous *Hitchcock*, this time making *Psycho* (1960), with the focus on his working and personal relationship with his wife, Alma (Helen Mirren). Neither film captured the life, loves or legacy of this extraordinary director. Both actors relied on prosthetics and vocal imitations instead of offering any real emotional insights.

6. Critical and commercial reception

Most biopics are either unalloyed hagiography, simple simpering over celebrity, or else the cinematic equivalent of kiss-and-tell tabloid exposes, concerned with just the sleaziest aspects of the life in question. – Andy Gill, *Word* (2004)

The biopic is an endlessly fascinating genre. Even its neglect raises issues about the values and preferences of scholars and journalists who dismiss the importance of the genre, as compared to the continued enthusiasm for biopics shown by the film artists who keep making them. – Dennis Bingham (2010: 27)

These two quotes articulate the contradictions that surround the bio-pic discourse. Despite accusations from critics that bio-pics are sensationalist, distorted or formulaic, viewers and award voters still embrace them.

And the award goes to...

Notoriously, the easiest way to win an Oscar is to play somebody bravely fighting a physical or mental handicap. The easiest route of all, in fact, is to play a gifted artist suddenly struck down by a disability. – Philip Hensher, *The Guardian* (2005)

Awards are often considered a yardstick for a film's success and an important element of their marketing strategy. If the actor has not been able to convince their peers that they have pulled it off, how can they convince the public? In recent cases, many of the Academy voters may have known some of the people being portrayed.

The first bio-pic to sweep up multiple awards was David Lean's epic *Lawrence of Arabia* (1962) starring Peter O'Toole as T. E. Lawrence. Other multiple award-winning films based on real personalities include *A Man for All Seasons* (1966), *Gandhi* (1982), *Amadeus* (1984), *Out of Africa* (1985), *The Last Emperor* (1987), *Schindler's List* (1993), *Braveheart* (1995), *A Beautiful Mind* (2001), *The King's Speech* (2010) and *12 Years a Slave* (2013). Not only are these all bio-pics, but they are also all bio-pics of heroes and/or those who have triumphed over great adversity. For the actor in question, they are often called to play a range of ages and emotions, while directors can capture a range of moods and tones. These facts, coupled with extremes of emotion and issues such as mental illness, has seen a high number of bio-pic-related Academy Award wins and nominations.

The Academy Awards, although not necessarily a marker of a film's quality, serves as a useful barometer against which one can gauge both public and industry approval of a film. Bio-pics have, understandably, been a consistent presence in the acting categories. This is a tradition that began in 1929 when George Arliss picked up an Academy Award for his portrayal of Benjamin Disraeli in *Disraeli* (1929). Tracing more recent nominations and wins, it is clear how important this genre has become in mainstream cinema. In 2004 three of the four actors nominated in the Best Actor category were for portrayals of real people. The award went to Jamie Foxx for his portrayal of Ray Charles in *Ray*, beating off Leonardo DiCaprio as Howard Hughes in *The Aviator,* Don Cheadle as Paul Rusesabagina in *Hotel Rwanda* and Johnny Depp as J. M. Barrie in *Finding Neverland*. The following year Philip Seymour Hoffman swooped up the award for his portrayal of Truman Capote, beating off two other bio-pic nominees, Joaquin Phoenix as Johnny Cash in *Walk the Line* and David Strathairn as Ed Morrow in *Good Night, and Good Luck*. In the Best Actress category Reese Witherspoon won for performance of Cash's wife June Carter, despite being up against tough bio-pic alumni, Judi Dench as Mrs Henderson in *Mrs. Henderson Presents* and Charlize Theron for Josey Aimes in the 'based on a true story' *North Country* (both previous bio-pic Academy Award winners with *Iris* and *Monster* respectively).

At award ceremonies across the globe in 2006, Forest Whitaker and Dame Helen Mirren were busy filling their mantelpieces with trophies for their roles of Idi Amin in *The Last King of Scotland* and Queen Elizabeth II in *The Queen*. So popular were bio-pics in 2007 that even foreign-language films were being represented. Marion Cotillard won for her portrayal of Edith Piaf in *La Vie en Rose*, whilst director Julian Schnabel was nominated for *The Diving Bell and the Butterfly*. Interestingly it was also a year of firsts with Cate Blanchett being nominated in both Best Actress and Best Supporting Actress categories for her roles as Elizabeth I in *Elizabeth: The Golden Age* and Bob Dylan in *I'm Not There*. Also the first time a woman was cast and nominated for playing a man.

True to recent form 2008 saw two acting giants going head-to-head with their portrayals of real-life political legends: Sean Penn as Harvey Milk in *Milk* triumphing over Frank Langella as Richard Nixon in *Frost/Nixon*. In 2009 Morgan Freeman received a nod for his role of Nelson Mandela in *Invictus*, and Sandra Bullock won for the semi-autobiographical *The Blind*

Side. Bullock's competition included Helen Mirren playing Sophia Tolstaya (Mrs Tolstoy) in *The Last Station* and Meryl Streep for Julia Child in *Julie & Julia*. In 2010 Colin Firth won for his portrayal of King George VI in *The King's Speech*, beating off Jesse Eisenberg as Mark Zuckerberg in *The Social Network* and James Franco as Aron Ralston in *127 Hours*. In 2011 Brad Pitt missed out on winning for his role of Billy Beane in *Moneyball*, Meryl Streep won for her portrayal of Margaret Thatcher in *The Iron Lady* and Michelle Williams was nominated for her Marilyn Monroe in *My Week with Marilyn*.

Then, 2012 saw Daniel Day-Lewis pick up his third Academy Award for *Lincoln*, his second for a bio-pic, having won in 1989 for *My Left Foot*. 2013 saw three of the five actors nominated for bio-pics: Chiwetel Ejiofor as Solomon Northup in *12 Years a Slave*, Leonardo DiCaprio as Jordan Belfort in *The Wolf of Wall Street*, with the award going to Matthew McConaughey for his performance as Ron Woodroof in *Dallas Buyers Club*.

This trend of award wins proves without doubt that films examining the lives of real people – whether they are singers, politicians, directors or writers – are a staple part of the filmic output of the industry.

Having established that bio-pics offer a vital commercial imperative in cinema today, particularly in Hollywood, the remainder of this book will focus on the films themselves. The films will be analysed within sub-genres based around the subject's profession and explored in terms of their production process, narrative structures, cultural value and critical responses.

1 THE SOUND OF MUSIC: SINGERS AND MUSICIANS TAKE CENTRE STAGE

Cinema is fascinated with rock stars. The trajectory of most music industry careers is the kind of rise and fall recommended by both Aristotle's *Poetics* and any cheap screenwriting manual you care to pick up. Hollywood likes large stories and mythic characters, which rockers by necessity are.

        – Toby Litt, *The New Statesman* (2007)

The writing and performing of music is both a visual and aural experience, the music's power driving the narrative forward with both diegetic and non-diegetic uses. Some films have required the actor to recreate the sounds of the singer in question: Kevin Spacey as Bobby Darin in *Beyond the Sea* (2004) and Joaquin Phoenix as Johnny Cash in *Walk the Line* whereas others have mimed to actual recordings: Marion Cotillard as Edith Piaf in *La Vie en Rose* and Jamie Foxx as Ray Charles in *Ray* – although he did so with his own piano playing. Some performances are so pitch perfect, such as Sam Riley as Ian Curtis in *Control*, that fans have questioned the actor's recreation, believing it to be mimed. Megan Good, vying for the coveted role of Whitney Houston, said, 'It's not about singing like her. You'd have to use her voice, you'd have to use her essence' (quoted in Anon. 2014). Music-based bio-pics were a popular sub-genre of the Hollywood Golden Age and have remained so. They provide a built-in fan base and opportunities for lucrative tie-in soundtrack sales.

The narrative structure of these music bio-pics can be seen as offering a contradiction to other emotion-driven dramas. In principle, the purpose of a narrative is to get from the beginning to the end of a story with the least amount of fuss. However, in a music bio-pic the narrative is constantly being interrupted by the songs. Within the bio-pic, the music can either be used on the soundtrack, as a work-in-progress, a fantasy sequence, re-viewed or as a finished performed musical routine. Sometimes these are used to support or clarify the subject's emotional status or as pure entertainment.

The three films explored here are *Ray*, *Beyond the Sea* and *I'm Not There* exploring the lives of three twentieth-century singers: Ray Charles, Bobby Darin and Bob Dylan. The narrative structure of the latter two relies on the audience having an appreciation of its generic predecessors, the more traditional cradle-to-grave approach as demostrated by the first.

Ray (2004)

Director: Taylor Hackford
Screenwriter: James L. White
Starring: Jamie Foxx (Ray Charles), Kerry Washington (Della Bea Washington) and Regina King (Margie Hendricks)
Subject: American musician, singer-songwriter and composer Ray Charles (Ray Charles Robinson, 1930 – 2004)

Ray Charles's son first approached Taylor Hackford in 1989 with the idea of turning his father's turbulent life into film. It would take fifteen years for the film to be financed. Hackford says, 'You have to understand I heard every-thing, from "nobody remembers Ray Charles," to "young people aren't interested," "African-American films don't sell overseas," and "biopics belong on television"' (quoted in Hamilos 2005).

The film's budget of $31 million was entirely raised by American entre-preneur, religious conservative and Ray Charles fan Philip Anschutz. He had initially requested that the film not feature any sex, swearing or drug taking. Hackford said, 'but this is a man who was a heroin addict for 20 years and slept with a different woman every night. I walked away from the project not once but twice, because [Anschutz] now had the rights and he was determined to make sure that it couldn't be an R-rated movie' (ibid.).

It was Ray Charles himself who convinced Hackford to find creative ways to show the darker underbelly of his life within the constraints imposed by Anschutz. Hackford rationalised that 'artists have been censored for centuries and still were able to communicate sex and everything else. It is ironic that a film like this should have been funded by a moral conservative. But he was straight about his beliefs and, once we agreed, he left me alone. That's much better than having somebody who believes they've got an artistic point of view, who tries to meddle with you' (ibid.).

The Charles family were involved throughout the development, filming and promotion process. Ray Charles saw a completed version of the film, but died before its release. Despite Hackford's belief that, 'in the end it's a sexy film and a tough film' (ibid.), David Ritz, co-author of Charles's autobiography, *Brother Ray: Ray Charles's Own Story* (2004), accused Hackford of sentimentalising the story and ignoring or downplaying the more unsavoury aspects of his life.

The film covers thirty years of Charles's life, from the mid-1930s when aged seven he witnesses his brother's death and goes blind, to the mid-1960s when he refused to play to a segregated audience in Georgia.

It opens in 1948 with the 17-year-old Ray boarding a greyhound bus to Seattle to seek a career as a nightclub pianist. The film follows a familiar rags-to-riches story as Charles's career takes off, his musical legacy displayed in performances of some his classics from the early solo hit 'Doin'

Jamie Foxx as Ray Charles in *Ray* (2004)

the Run Around', to his popular hits 'Hit the Road Jack' and 'Unchain my Heart', to the song that changed history, 'Georgia on My Mind'. Jamie Foxx, who lost 30lbs for the role, was a classically trained pianist and plays his own piano throughout, whilst lip-synching to the Charles originals.

The film does not shy away from the darker side showing Charles as a flawed man – cheating on his wife; humiliating his loyal friends; dumping Atlantic Records who nurtured his talent and turned him into a star; and his addiction to heroin. As Andy Gill writes, 'Ray manages to present its subject as a complex, multi-faceted character, capable of both brilliant musical innovation and a ruthless attitude that sometimes bordered on cruelty (2004: 58).

Hackford's decision to employ flashbacks to expose the childhood tragedies that plague the adult man psychologically underpins the narrative. Flashbacks of Charles's poor upbringing, his young brother's death, his sudden blindness, being sent to a special school for the blind and his mother's death soon afterwards, are incorporated into the 1948–1966 timeline as incidents in the present recall tragedies from his past. Showing that despite his successes, these personal demons haunted Ray until he sought solace in heroin and womanising (he fathered twelve children out of wedlock).

By stopping the film two-thirds of the way through Charles's life and at a moment of triumph (having kicked his heroin habit), it endorses Charles's view of his life. In an interview shortly before his death on the film's release, he said, 'I've had some wonderful things happen to me, but I've had some pretty dramatic things to happen to me, too. I would like people to know that you can recover from a lot of adversity that you might have in your life if you keep pressing on ... In other words, you don't give up just because you get knocked down a few times' (quoted in Gill 2004). The omission of Charles's last forty years fails to show his continued womanising (leading to his divorce) and decline in commercial popularity.

The film was a success at the box office, earning $20 million over its opening weekend. It went on to make $75 million. It was nominated for six Academy Awards including Best Picture, and won two: Best Actor for Jamie Foxx and Best Sound. The last album Charles recorded was held back to coincide with the film's release.

The critical response to the film was largely positive with critics highlighting Foxx's uncanny recreation of Ray Charles, for example:

Jamie Foxx suggests the complexities of Ray Charles in a great, exuberant performance. What [he] gets just right is the physical Ray Charles, and what an extrovert he was. Foxx so accurately reflects my own images and memories of Charles that I abandoned thoughts of how much 'like' Charles he was and just accepted him as Charles, and got on with the story. (Ebert 2004a)

Its detractors questioned the tone, and the judicious selection and presentation of the major life incidents:

It's got that award-friendly disabled angle and a cheery thumbs up to race relations, as well as bags of personal hell (heroin, adultery, flashbacks) that always seems to go hand in hand with professional virtuosity. While the music in *Ray* is ear-tingingly good, the biggest noise is the scratch of boxes being ticked. (Shoard 2005)

Beyond the Sea (2004)

Director: Kevin Spacey
Screenwriters: Kevin Spacey and Lewis Colick
Starring: Kevin Spacey (Bobby Darin) and Kate Bosworth (Sandra Dee)
Subject: American singer and actor Bobby Darin (Waldon Robert Cassotto, 1936–1973).

This was a personal project for Kevin Spacey who was a big fan of Bobby Darin and wanted to reclaim him as the great star he had been, but was now largely forgotten in favour of other entertainers of that period. Spacey had featured Darin numbers in the previous film he had starred in, *Midnight in the Garden of Good of Evil* (1997). When the rights became available, after an earlier aborted film helmed by Barry Levinson fell through, Spacey worked with Darin's son Dodd to acquire them.

Beyond the Sea depicts Darin's childhood, rise to success in both the music and film industries during the 1950s and 1960s, his marriage/break-up with Sandra Dee and his death aged 37.

The film does not employ a straightforward narrative structure, favouring a more knowing deconstruction and examination of a 'traditional' bio-pic: a film within a film. The film opens as many music bio-pics do, at a moment of glory, Darin at the peak of his career on stage at the Copacabana nightclub. The camera pulls back to reveal that we are actually on a sound stage. The adult Darin is confronted by himself as a young boy, arguing that he's 'gotten it all wrong'.

The narrative moves back and forth in time, with versions of his childhood and adult self, articulating a schism Darin himself felt. Spacey stated, 'Bobby Darin said he always felt like two different people. That Waldon Robert Cassotto spent half his life trying to become Bobby Darin, and Bobby Darin spent the rest of his life trying to get back to Waldon Robert Cassotto' (quoted in Murray 2004). The question of identity is central to both the film and Darin himself, who discovered late in life that his 'sister' was really his mother, and that his 'parents' were his grandparents.

This emotional crisis is shown through the older and younger versions of Darin interacting with one another. In the film's closing number, after Darin's death, the two dance, within an ensemble of Darins. Spacey said, 'Bobby went off the rails, and I think it took him awhile to put it back together. That's sort of what I try to do in the last dance sequence ... you have all of these representative Bobby's, all these dancers, and they all become one. Finally he's sort of figured out how to put it together' (ibid.).

The traditional beat points of the rise and successes in film, music and television career are all covered. His poor health as a child becomes a recurring motif as ill-health in adulthood plagues his work and personal life. His marriage to the much younger film star Sandra Dee and their marriage break-up, is shown in the style of a Hollywood movie. When he marries Dee he jokingly tells this bubbly blonde-haired all-American girl, 'You're not Audrey Hepburn'. Later, when they are filming in Italy, they are seen riding vespas à la Hepburn and Gregory Peck in *Roman Holiday* (1953).

The film's examination of the genre is further revealed when, as part of Darin's success, there are plans to film 'a self-portrait on film', leading to discussions of how it should be structured, which adds a pleasing postmodern dimension highlighting and exposing some of the problems inherent in the genre. Perhaps, as a knowing nod to Spacey's actual age of 45 (playing a man who died at 37), there are quips about Darin himself being too old to play the screen version of himself. Darin's father/grandfather, Charlie Cassotto Maffia (Bob Hoskins), responds, 'How can you to be too old to play yourself?'

Kevin Spacey as Bobby Darin and Kate Bosworth as Sandra Dee in *Beyond the Sea* (2004)

There are arguments as to how the film within the film should start. The first idea tried is that of Darin's talent manager, Stephen Blauner (John Goodman): 'It should start with a kid playing Bobby as a child – a mini version and he's a method actor.' This version starts and is then scrapped. 'So how do you think we should start?' asks Blauner of Darin. 'If you want some truth. I'll give you some truth.' Darin clicks his fingers. 'This is where would should start, on the street where I grew up. Back to the beginning.' The older Darin is now watching the childhood scenes, much like Scrooge in Dickens' *A Christmas Carol*. Darin (in voice over): '… a world I could live in – the whole street dancing – they didn't dance down the street like that – it was just a fantasy sequence. Memories are moonbeams, we can do with them what we want.' This line about moonbeams and fantasy dancing sequences urges the audience to accept this version of Darin's life primarily as entertainment with the factual document second.

The film received mixed reviews when it opened, with critics focusing on Spacey's complete involvement in the project and his obsession with the now all-but-forgotten Darin:

> This vainglorious biopic about Bobby Darin is really about what the '60s pop singer and actor means to Kevin Spacey, who co-produces, co-writes, directs, stars in, dances and sings his way through this movie. To be fair, Spacey's rendition of Darin is right on the imitative money. He sings the entire soundtrack, almost nuance for nuance, like Darin. But the movie never goes beyond Spacey's parlor tricks. (Thomson 2004)

The movie is an extraordinary one-man show: Mr. Spacey is not only the star and a producer, but also director, co-writer and leader of a 19-piece band that will tour nine cities, backing his Darin act. Mr. Spacey, with the help of seven toupees and the make-up team from *The Lord of the Rings*, essentially becomes Bobby Darin in the film. (McDougal 2004)

The movie possesses genuine feeling because Spacey is there with Darin during all the steps of this journey, up and down, all the way into death. Not all stories have happy endings. Not all lives have third acts. (Ebert 2004b)

I'm Not There (2007)

Director: Todd Haynes
Screenwriters: Todd Haynes and Oren Moverman
Starring: Cate Blanchett, Richard Gere, Heath Ledger, Ben Wishaw, Christian
    Bale and Marcus Carl Franklin as versions of Bob Dylan
Subject: American musician, singer-songwriter, artist and writer Bob Dylan
    (Robert Allen Zimmerman, 1941–present)

The poster proclaims that 'Christian Bale, Cate Blanchett, Marcus Carl Franklin, Richard Gere, Heath Ledger and Ben Wishaw are all Bob Dylan', clearly promoting *I'm Not There* as a 'Bob Dylan film'. An on-screen disclaimer states that *I'm Not There* is 'inspired by the music and the many lives of Bob Dylan'. Yet these are the film's only references to Bob Dylan, other than the music sources. Bob Dylan endorsed the film by giving Haynes the right use his music – a first. Both original and new versions of the Dylan songs are used.

For over fifty years Dylan has pushed musical boundaries. He has transformed folk singer and author of anthemic protest songs, to rocker and finally icon. However, the man himself remains enigmatic.

I'm Not There is no birth-to-death bio-pic that will reveal the man behind the icon status; this is an elegiac love letter to Dylan, flitting back and forward in time to focus on aspects of his career, music and life decisions. To further complicate this temporal structure, six actors play different versions of Dylan from various periods of his life. True to the film's title, Bob

Dylan is not there. These six impressions, six sides, six characters must surely be inspired by Luigi Pirandello's meta-physical play *Six Character in Search of an Author* (1921) about the relationship between authors, their characters and theatrical devices.

Through these versions of Dylan the film focuses on the first two decades of his output from the late 1950s to the late 1970s. This film does not tell Dylan's story *per se*, but re-interprets profound incidents and periods from his life, taking direct quotes to create a complex narrative structure, that is also a thought-provoking meditation on celebrity and its impact on the life.

The film's director, Todd Haynes, explains his approach saying, 'Every biopic has the same story. The personal side suffers from a public life – not really that unique. The only true and honest way to approach Dylan's story for contemporary viewers who seem to know most of the key events in his life was to reproduce that sense of shock' (quoted in Silberg 2007). Haynes is deconstructing not just the life of Bob Dylan but the public's changing/ changed attitude to celebrities. The film's title was taken from a 1967 song recorded, but never released, until its use here.

The production notes for the film outline its vision: '*I'm Not There* is a film that dramatizes the life and music of Bob Dylan as a series of shifting personae, each performed by a different actor – poet, prophet, outlaw, fake, star of electricity, rock and roll, martyr born-again Christian – seven identities braided together, seven organs pumping through one life story' (*Weinstein Company* 2007). A seventh character, a version of Charlie Chaplin, was in the original script but not filmed. The film begins with a narration (by Kris Kristofferson) which mirrors this vision. Each character's world is defined by its visual look, created by cinematographer Edward Lachman.

The film opens with a point-of-view shot, placing the audience in the shoes of Jude Quinn (Cate Blanchett) as he is ushered through the back stage area and on to the stage at a mid-1960s folk festival. The Jude sequences, shot in 35mm black and white, draw heavily on D. A. Pennebaker's documentary *Dont Look Back* (1967) which followed Dylan on tour in 1965/66. It also echoes the hand-held experimental European New Wave films of the period by Richard Lester and Federico Fellini. Flash frames and point-of-view shots exemplify Jude's celebrity besiegement. Jude is Dylan at his most famous, most interesting and most outspoken. At the peak of his fame in 1965/66,

Cate Blanchett as Jude Quinn in *I'm Not There* (2007)

he caused controversy by playing an electric guitar rather than the expected acoustic at a folk festival and was booed, leading to his original fans' accusations that he had sold-out. The film features a surreal dream sequence in which Jude guns down the entire concert audience who booed him for this change. The Jude character offers the most closely accurate portrayal of Dylan and the most easily recognisable version. The conceit of casting a woman to play it is perhaps why Blanchett's performance was singled out by critics and received the acting award nominations and wins.

The 1950s version (shot on 35mm colour) is an allusion to Dylan's obsession with the folk/blues singer Woody Guthrie. Woody (Marcus Carl Franklin) is a child out time and place: an eleven-year-old African-American child in America of the 1950s, but riding boxcars right out of the Great Depression of the 1930s. Having escaped a juvenile detention centre, he is befriended by Mrs. Arvin who advises Woody to, 'Live your own time, child, sing about your own time.'

Jack Rollins (Christian Bale) is a young Greenwich Village political folk musician of the 1960s. His story is told in the style of a period black-and-white 16mm documentary, with interviews from people who knew him giving their commentary on his transition from Jack Rollins to Born Again Christian, Pastor John, singing gospel music. Rollins is praised as an anthemic protest singer and is shown drunkenly accepting an award and insulting the audience and claiming that he saw something of himself in JFK's assassin Lee Harvey Oswald. Rollins's acceptance uses elements of a speech Dylan gave when accepting the Tom Paine Award from the National Emergency Civil Liberties Committee in December 1963.

Heath Ledger plays the hip 1970s Hollywood film star Robbie Clark, best known for his performance in the Jack Rollins bio-pic (ie a bio-pic about the fictional Bob Dylan as played by Christian Bale). This is the most domestic portion of the film showing a version of Dylan's own difficult marriage and divorce to Sarah Lownds, here represented as Claire (Charlotte Gainsbourg). These sequences are shot in 35mm in the style of the American New Wave, making use of real locations, natural lighting, unmotivated camera moves and unbalanced framing.

Ben Wishaw's character shares the same name as the French poet Arthur Rimbaud who Dylan much admired, and who was an icon for 1960s radical artists. His comments on events are given expressionlessly, direct to camera. The effect of the grainy black and white is as though he is being interrogated by an off-screen interviewer.

The final version is of an aged outlaw, Billy Reed (Richard Gere), portraying the ageing Bob Dylan as Billy the Kid in a Wild West sequence who defeats the older Pat Garrett (Bruce Greenwood). Here, Billy is shown as an outlaw trying to find refuge from a corrupt world. The sequence references Dylan's self-imposed exile after his 1966 motorcycle crash, as shown in the Jude Quinn sections. It also draws attention to Dylan's acting role of Alias in *Pat Garrett and Billy the Kid* (Sam Peckinpah, 1973), in which Billy was played by Kris Kristofferson, *I'm Not There*'s unseen narrator. These sequences are shot in 35mm, in the style of movies of the period like *Butch Cassidy and the Sundance Kid* (George Roy Hill, 1969) and *McCabe and Mrs. Miller* (Robert Altman, 1971).

The film ends with real concert footage of Bob Dylan playing a harmonica solo from the 1965/66 tour, shot by D. A. Pennebaker.

I'm Not There is disorientating, challenging, provocative, teasing and electric. Haynes says:

I just wanted to make a film about Dylan in a way that used the cinematic medium to get close to something that I think is really true about him. Which is that he refuses to stay in one category, doing the same kind of music, fulfilling the same expectations. You don't have to understand every reference because music is an intensely emotional, primarily visceral medium, and I think film is too. John Lennon said about Dylan, you don't have to understand a single word he says to know what he's talking about. (Quoted in Dalton 2007)

I'm Not There is an ambitious film, which failed to find a wide audience on its release, taking only $11 million at the box office world-wide. It received mixed reviews:

> Todd Haynes's hotly anticipated *I'm Not There* seems to take pride in what it is not. It's not a straight biopic, not a rock movie, not a proper narrative, not a love letter, not a crowd-pleaser, not even a film that mentions the name 'Bob Dylan'. Not a lot of fun? Well, that's a moot point. It is an ambitiously conceived and lovingly textured piece of work, a movie of images and distorted facts that will hang about your consciousness long after you've seen it. (Quinn 2007b)

Blanchett's performance was particularly singled out in reviews and in award circles:

> Cate Blanchett is the movie's jewel, and also its problem. It was great casting, and her eerily exact inhabiting of Dylan's mannerisms is an inspired alienation effect. Whenever she is not on screen, however, the voltage-level drops, and her presence has the unfortunate effect of making the male contribution look ordinary. Yet if Blanchett had been the only Dylan on screen, it might have looked like an overstretched gimmick. Haynes has pitched her at the right length: a super-strength cameo. Her Dylan is intelligent, confident, artificial in the best sense: a strong contender for the big awards, and a good reason to see the film. (Bradshaw 2007c)

> A riddle wrapped in a mystery inside an enigma, *I'm Not There* is essentially a homage from one fiercely single-minded artist to another. Whatever its flaws, it is bold, beautiful and commendably ambitious. (Dalton 2007)

Further viewing

Behind the Candelabra (Steven Soderbergh, 2013); Liberace (Michael Douglas)
Control (Anton Corijn, 2007); Ian Curtis (Sam Riley)

De-Lovely (Irwin Winkler, 2004); Cole Porter (Kevin Kline)

Gainsbourg: A Heroic Life (Joann Sfar, 2010); Serge Gainsbourg (Eric Elmosnino)

Notorious (George Tillman jr, 2009); The Notorious B.I.G. (Jamal Woolard)

Nowhere Boy (Sam Taylor-Wood, 2009); John Lennon (Aaron Johnson)

Sex & Drugs & Rock & Roll (Matt Whitecross, 2010); Ian Drury (Andy Serkis)

Shine (Scott Hicks, 1997); David Helfgott (Geoffrey Rush)

Telstar: The Joe Meek Story (Nick Moran, 2009); Joe Meek (Con O'Neill)

La Vie en Rose (Olivier Dahan (2007); Edit Piaf (Marion Cotillard)

Walk the Line (James Mangold, 2005); Johnny Cash (Joaquin Phoenix)

2   HOLLYWOODLAND: ACTORS AND DIRECTORS
AS PORTRAYED BY ACTORS AND DIRECTORS

> While the entertainment bio-film may not possess as voluminous
> a body of completed productions as other immediately recogniz-
> able genres, it nevertheless is firmly established. The reflexive
> impulse, to construct works of entertainment about entertainers
> themselves, seems to be as strong as it ever was ... and is likely to
> persist. – Robert Milton Miller (1983: 361)

From the earliest flickering black-and-white images on a wall, to modern-
day blockbusters, Hollywood as a dream factory (not necessarily a geo-
graphic space) has fascinated audiences. Filmmakers have responded to
this by producing films about their own industry. It is a business that on
the surface is all glitz and glamour – but what lies beneath is something
much darker. The more successful films about 'Hollywood' tend to explore
and explode the myth of the 'dream factory'. The stars chosen for bio-pics
are often ones who have become tarnished by gossip, or have suffered at
the hands of the industry itself.

  These films offer us a glimpse of what lies behind the cameras, how
this powerful industry works, and how they have re-told their own past. The
three case studies here focus on the film career of Ed Wood, hailed as the
worst film director ever; film and aviation mogul Howard Hughes; and the
little-known (outside the US) 1960s TV star Bob Crane. Through their striking visual style, narrative structure and performances, these films offer
insights into the lives of these troubled men.

Ed Wood (1994)

Director: Tim Burton
Screenwriters: Larry Karaszewski and Scott Alexander
Starring: Johnny Depp (Ed Wood) and Martin Landau (Bela Lugosi)
Subject: American screenwriter, director, producer, actor, author and film
   editor Ed Wood (Edward Davis "Ed" Wood Jr, 1924 – 1978)

Bio-pics about Hollywood stars are fairly common, those about the creative forces behind the screen less so. It is therefore surprising that one of the first and most significant in the mid-1990s renaissance was not one of the great directors from the canon, but one whose reputation rests on having directed what is often considered to be one of the worst films of all time *Plan 9 From Outer Space* (1956).

   Screenwriters Karaszewski and Alexander's source material for the screenplay was Rudolph Grey's *Nightmare of Ecstasy: The Life and Art of Edward D. Wood, Jr* (1992). This led to Wood's films being shown on late night television in the US, which brought about a renewed interest in this minor-league film director in the early 1990s. For his book Grey interviewed the surviving members of Wood's troupe and recorded all the conflicting accounts of the man, the films and the filmmaking process. Karaszewski says, 'What we were attracted to about Ed was the incredible, charismatic optimism he seemed to have. It almost didn't matter whether the movies were any good; he just wanted to make movies so badly and wanted to have all his friends in them' (quoted in Warren 1994: 34).

   Karaszewski and Alexander had achieved commercial success with *Problem Child* (1990) and *Problem Child 2* (1991), yet wanted to work on something that would have a greater critical resonance. They returned to an idea Alexander had had in 1983, an Ed Wood bio-pic then entitled *The Man in the Angora Sweater,* and began work on a speculative script. They approached director Michael Lehmann, who in turn went to producer Denise Di Novi who was then working with Burton. It transpired that Burton, noting parallels between his and Wood's passion for film, wanted to direct it. Lehmann stepped aside.

   Burton said, 'I hate most biopics. I find they are really stodgy and boring, because people take a much too reverential approach, and it's fake. What's great about *Ed Wood* is that it's rough; it's not like a completely hardcore, realistic biopic. I'm only taking the spirit of what I think some of this stuff is and trying to project a certain kind of feeling' (quoted in Salisbury 1994). Given Burton's empathy for Wood, the film does not mock, but celebrates Wood as a determined filmmaker – one that so loves movies, particularly his own, that he fails to see how bad they are.

The film focuses on a few years in Wood's life, using a linear narrative structure. The setting is Hollywood in the 1950s (and the film is shot in black and white to mirror this period). Wood is a wannabe director/star/writer making a series of (really) low-budget movies with no scripts, sets, costumes or functioning actors. Scenes from his films, *Glen and Glenda* (1953), *Bride of the Monster* (1955) and *Plan 9 From Outer Space* are all lovingly restaged. Wood remains incredibly optimistic, unfazed by disasters, financial problems, interfering producers. For some, he secured funding from his local Baptist Church, who insisted the entire cast be baptised.

Yet the film is more than one horror movie fan paying homage to another. It also examines Wood's relationship with the women in his life and, centrally, his relationship with the ageing Lugosi. Burton says, 'People think it's funny that I did this movie. It's like because I've been successful, why would I want to make a movie about somebody who's not successful? But the way I feel about that and him and me is that any of the movies could go either way, they really could, and that line between success and failure is a very thin one' (ibid.).

Parallels between Burton and Wood are numerous. Ed Wood employed one of his horror heroes Bela Lugosi in his films, and Lugosi's last screen appearance was in a Wood production. As a filmmaker just starting out, Burton managed to get his idol Vincent Price to narrate one of his early short films, *Vincent* (1982) and Price's last on-screen appearance was as the inventor in Burton's *Edward Scissorhands* (1990).

The film shows a genuine friendship between Lugosi (Martin Landau), a morphine addicted has-been, and Wood (Johnny Depp) who is both exploiting the star while also giving his last years meaning. Lugosi had been a major star of the Universal horror films in the 1930s, but by the 1950s he had been abandoned. Despite being in terrible pain and using morphine and alcohol as props, he always turned up for work and gave his all, until the end. He died during the shooting *Plan 9 From Outer Space*.

Bela Lugosi Jr, a Los Angeles lawyer, was unhappy with the portrayal of his father and said, 'I read enough of the script to decide that he wasn't portrayed either accurately or respectfully, and so I stopped reading' (quoted in Clark 1994: 91).

The film ends on a high-point with a premiere of *Plan 9 of Outer Space* in 1959: an occurrence that eluded the original film. By ending here, the film does not follow the real Wood's descent into pornography.

The film's original title, *The Man in the Angora Sweater*, drew attention to Wood's transvestism. By changing it to *Ed Wood*, the film is now aligned more closely to biography where instant recognition of the subject is placed above the poetic. The publicity material for the film featured images of Depp in a combination of male and female clothing, lounging in a director's chair, megaphone in hand, offering a quick summary of his personal and professional world's in a shared space. The film starts during the production of his début feature film *Glen and Glenda*. Wood himself played the film's central crossdressing character as a way of 'coming out' to his girlfriend Delores Fuller (Sarah Jessica Parker) about his transvestisism. She was unable to accept this side of him, and broke up. Wood's next girlfriend, who he would later marry, Kathy (Patricia Arquette) was comfortable with this side of the man. The two women met for the first time on the set for *Ed Wood*. Johnny Depp confidently recreates this ambiguity of a virile good looking heterosexual man complete with Clark Gable moustache striding around the studio in knee length pencil skirts, high-heel shoes and tight-fitting angora sweaters.

The film is peopled with genuine characters and incidents, as well as fabricating others that could have happened, including the scene where Wood, dejected by production problems, bumps into Orson Welles (Vincent D'Onofrio) who gives him a pep-talk ending with the wise words, 'visions are worth fighting for'. Burton comments:

> I liked these people, I enjoyed the idea of them. I liked that they were all completely out of it and everybody thought they were doing the greatest things, and they weren't. There's just something very appealing about people who go out on a limb, who are perceived by society to be something else, so therefore in some ways that loosens them up to just be themselves. (Quoted in Salisbury 1994)

The film opened to enthusiastic reviews, but failed to recoup its $18 million budget at the box office.

Johnny Depp as Ed Wood and Mike Starr as producer Georgie Weiss in *Ed Wood* (1994)

Burton's biopic of the man often described as the world's worst filmmaker may offer a somewhat favourably distorted account of the man and his films – it ends before his slide into porn, penury and alcoholism and, while recreating certain scenes from Wood's work with astonishing accuracy, manages to avoid showing his most tiresomely nonsensical sequences – but it certainly succeeds as a funny, touching tribute to tenacity, energy, ambition and friendship. Affection shines through warm and bright, aided no end by Stefan Czapsky's evocative b/w camerawork, and by a host of spot-on lookalike performances. (Andrew 2006a)

Dennis Bingham in *Whose Lives Are They Anyway?* dedicates a chapter to *Ed Wood*. Under the chapter heading 'The Biopic of Someone Undeserving' he states:

Ed Wood presents a comic paradox: a biopic hero who has everything – enthusiasm, optimism, compassion in his befriending of faded star Bela Lugosi … loyalty to his friends and co-workers, tenacity, and something he wanted to say in films. He has everything, that is, expect talent. … In casting an affectionate look at a passionate failure, the film parodies the biopic genre, not by imitating the genre in order to ridicule it, but by inverting the values on which it is based. (2010: 147)

The Aviator (2004)

Director: Martin Scorsese
Screenwriter: John Logan
Starring: Leonardo DiCaprio (Howard Hughes), Cate Blanchett (Katharine
    Hepburn), Kate Beckinsale (Ava Gardner), Jude Law (Errol Flynn) and
    Gwen Stefani (Jean Harlow)
Subject: American Mogul, filmmaker, inventor, pilot, playboy and eccentric
    billionaire Howard Hughes (Howard Robard Hughes, Jr. 1905 – 1976)

John Logan drew inspiration for his screenplay from Charles Higham's popular biography *Howard Hughes* (1993). Michael Mann was originally on board as director, but the experience of *Ali* had left him unwilling to commit to another bio-pic at this time. He stayed on as producer when Martin Scorsese took over as director. The film's budget was $110 million and shooting took place over five months, predominantly in Canada.

The Aviator covers two decades of Howard Hughes's life from the late 1920s to the mid-1940s. Its focus is on Hughes's achievements in the fields of aviation and movies, and on his descent into paranoia and obsessive–compulsive behaviour. It skips the traditional opening credits, or familiar opening at a moment of glory to show a brief scene of a young boy, aged nine, being bathed by his mother. Suddenly we are in the middle of the airfield, with planes flying overhead. It is now 1927 and Hughes (aged 22) in movie-mogul mode is making an impact on the Hollywood landscape with his World War I flying epic, *Hell's Angels*. It ends shortly after the successful flight of the Hercules in 1947.

Hell's Angels was to be his masterpiece of the silent cinema. At a cost of $4m, it took three years to make. When *The Jazz Singer* (1927) was released he remade it as a sound film at even more expense and it was finally released in 1930. The film lost $1.5 million but was well received. His biggest hit was *Scarface* (1932), a portrayal of gangster Al Capone that brought such a level of violence and glamour to the screen that it was instrumental in the introduction of the notorious Hays Production Code that dominated Hollywood for the next three decades.

Restless and rich he moves on to his own flying projects – breaking records, designing and building aircraft and establishing his own airline, TWA, as well as wooing the *crème de le crème* of the Hollywood A-list

Leonard diCaprio as Howard Hughes on the set of Hell's Angels in *The Aviator* (2004)

including Katharine Hepburn and Ava Gardner. In these early sequences Hughes is sleek, charming and alive.

The pivotal event that brings about his steady descent into madness is his 1946 near-fatal plane crash into the rooftops of a Beverly Hills suburb. Although he did not physically crash and burn, this incident was the catalyst for a thirty-year decline. Although the film's narrative ends a year later in 1947, his final diminished years are hinted at here, as he starts his downward trajectory into madness and reclusiveness.

There are further brief flashbacks to his childhood which serves as an explanation for his increasingly destructive behaviour in his relationships with women and hygiene. These sequences were added by screenwriter Logan and are not in Higham's biography, although his mother's fear that he could contract typhus and her obsession with quarantining him, refusing to let him play with other children fearing they would pass on diseases, is well-documented.

The film treats his paranoia and obsessive-compulsive disorder (OCD) with sympathy and pathos. His OCD manifested in extreme obsession with cleanliness, and washing his hands is shown through extreme close-ups of a bathroom doorknob looming large, with Hughes waiting for someone else to come in to prevent him from having to touch it.

He locks himself away to hide from his increasing deafness (caused by the accident). A scene where a naked Hughes sits on his germ-free seat watching his old movies reflected onto his naked torso encapsulates all his obsessions (both positive and negative) in one haunting image. This is the birth of the babbling demented recluse that was to define him, a variation on which is depicted in *Melvin and Howard* (Jonathan Demme, 1980).

Scorsese uses film stock, shooting and editing styles appropriate to the historical period and Hughes's mental decline. The film's pre-1935 scenes are shown in shades of red and cyan blue with green objects appearing blue. This was done to emulate the look of early colour films shot using the 'multicolor' process (which Hughes owned). For the remainder of the film, post-1935, they appear saturated, mirroring those of the three-strip Technicolor process of the period. Towards the end of the film, when Hughes locks himself away, the *mise-en-scène* becomes darker, as he sits alone in the shadows.

Scorsese stated:

It kept reminding me of Greek mythology and the curse of the family and how they deal with it. I was thinking about the Minotaur and the labyrinth. Basically through his whole life Hughes is trying to escape the labyrinth, but he's the labyrinth. ... Howard Hughes at this point in his life, his flaw, the curse so to speak, is the curse for all of us in terms of a nation, a country that acquires wealth like empires. I love studying ancient history and seeing how empires rise and fall. They sow the seeds of their own destruction and I think that's what fascinated me. Ultimately the story asks, is that the wave of the future for everyone? (Film4 2004a)

Scorsese would return to the pioneers of film history in *Hugo* (2011) which features Ben Kingsley as the pioneering special effects film director Georges Méliès.

The film won great critical acclaim and was rewarded with box office and awards success. It was nominated for eleven Academy Awards, and won five.

The Aviator ends brilliantly on an image that's tragic, moving and kind of brave; Hughes, gripped by another panic attack and accompanying Tourette's-like verbal spasm, repeats "the way of the future" relentlessly into a coldly unresponsive washroom mirror. It's 1947 and Howard Hughes is just 42. We know, as we watch the trauma in the washroom, that the way of the future for him was a long, dreadful contraction into a nightmarish isolation. The fact that you really, genuinely care is probably *The Aviator*'s strongest recommendation of all. (Maconie 2005: 114)

Auto Focus (2002)

Director: Paul Schrader
Screenwriter: Michael Gerbosi
Starring: Greg Kinnear (Bob Crane), Rita Wilson (Anne Crane) and Willem Dafoe (John Henry Carpenter)
Subject: American actor and disc jockey Bob Crane (Robert Edward 'Bob' Crane, 1928–1978)

Auto Focus was co-produced by screenwriters Larry Karaszewski and Scott Alexander. They have found success specialising in bio-pics of minor players, offering private views of these public personas: cult movie director Ed Wood, Hustler magazine publisher Larry Flynt (Woody Harrelson) in *The People vs Larry Flynt* (1996) and TV star Andy Kaufman (Jim Carrey) in *Man on the Moon* (1999). These are what Alexander describes as, 'anti-biopics ... biopics about people who don't deserve one ... They're attractive because they're so impassioned and they're fighting a big wave that's about to crash down on them. It makes for colourful characters and that's more fun than a noble character' (2002).

Screenwriter Michael Gerbosi and producer Todd Rosken used the true-crime cop procedural *The Murder of Bob Crane: Who Killed the Star of Hogan's Heroes?* (1993) by Robert Graysmith as their starting point. Graysmith had been one of the reporters working at the *San Francisco Chronicle* in 1969 when the Zodiac killings took place. His first-hand account of this was used as the basis of *Zodiac* (David Fincher, 2007). In 1996, with the rights to the book procured, Gerbosi and Rosken began turning Graysmith's book into a screenplay. In 1998, they met with Karaszewski and Alexander who advised throwing out the book's police procedural structure, which only saw Crane's life in flashback, and to focus instead on Crane himself. According to Gerbosi, Karaszewski and Alexander said 'they focused on the few years of a person's life that mattered. These cradle-to-grave biopics are too broad and don't really get underneath the surface. So I picked the years that I thought mattered, a handful where events started to overwhelm Bob, and began him on the spiral to where he wound up (quoted in Ferreyra 2003).

In 1999, with the script finished, and Karaszewski and Alexander now on board as producing partners, the search began for financing for a project with seemingly little commercial appeal. Gerbosi has noted how, '... many of the independents – the place the three [of us] thought would go gung-ho for a project like this – passed one after the other. In the end, though, Sony liked the project enough to put *Auto Focus* into production' (Ferreyra 2003).

With Greg Kinnear secured as star and Paul Schrader directing, filming began in 2001. It now focused on Bob Crane who, at the film's start, seemingly has it all: he is the star of the hit TV sitcom *Hogan's Heroes* (1965–1971), married to his childhood sweetheart, with three children. Behind the façade is a man addicted to sex, pornography and later recording his sex acts using the latest video recording technology. The film follows this downward spiral from churchgoing family man in 1965, through his divorce and second marriage, increasing reliance on sex and alcohol, to his murder in 1978 (which remains unsolved).

The film opens in the mid-1960s and Crane's voice-over tells us 'I'm a likeable guy' and so it appears. In this bright, sunny Los Angeles Crane is shown hosting a light-hearted morning radio show, wearing pastel patterned jumpers; and keen to exploit his 'Jack Lemmon' likeability in films. Anxious to break into acting he accepts the title role of Colonel Robert Hogan in *Hogan's Heroes*, set in a Nazi POW camp. Its success makes him a TV star, and draws attraction from a bevy of female fans. Through a co-star he meets John 'Carpy' Carpenter who introduces him to the early portable video cameras. Hogan's sex addiction starts off with the soft-core magazines and progresses to the point that Hogan is starring in his own sex movies. When *Hogan's Heroes* is axed, he finds increasing solace in this world.

As Crane's life deteriorates so does the look of the film, mirroring both his mood but also the transition from all-American family guy and the high values of a network TV show to the grainy underbelly of 1970s video quality and the sleazy nightclubs he and Carpenter haunt. From careful and straightforward sitcom cinematography to the jitteriness associated with hand-held, this visual deterioration echoes his mental transformation from wholesome family man to washed-out paranoiac. This is a film that travels from the glamour to the gutter, visually and narratively.

The neat compartmentalisation of Crane's two lives collides in a fantasy sequence mid-way through the film, signalling the change in him and

Greg Kinnear as Bob Crane in a dream sequence from *Auto Focus* (2002)

the visual and aural tone for the film's second half. Hungover, Crane is on set and his mind wanders as he imagines that the set is now a real prison. His co-star Patricia Olson (Maria Bello) with whom he is having an affair (and would later marry) appears in her usual costume, but strips down to reveal provocative lingerie and begins to seduce him and the other Nazi officers. His wife Anne (Rita Wilson) appears looking demure and vulgarly gives him permission to stray. His children beg him to stay. He is snapped back to reality by the director calling out.

Fred Murphy's cinematography (use of film stocks, camera move-ments/angles and lighting), is enhanced by Christina Boden's increasingly agitated editing, and composer's Angelo Badalamenti creepy score. These visual and aural signposts aid the audience's reading of Crane. Crane him-self remains an enigma, curiously dispassionate, his voice-over narrative adding no insights into the psyche; it is a bland soundtrack to a man who seemingly has no emotional engagement with the world in which he has become embroiled. There is plenty of nudity, but this is not a sexy film. The sex is joyless, and his and Carpenter's re-viewing of their exploits does not seem anything more than a technical experience as though the mechanics of the technology is of greater importance than the act it is recoding. All this provides 'a deep portrait of a shallow man, lonely and empty, going through the motions of having a good time' (Ebert 2002).

Despite being well-received critically it did little business at the box office, largely due to the fact that neither Bob Crane nor Greg Kinnear had high-profiles outside of the US at this time and the film's subject matter was a tough one.

> Paul Schrader does biopics like no other director, choosing the most lurid and disastrous subjects ... [This] is a splendidly taut example of the genre [which is] at first like a singular meditation on a very individual man's unique obsession with the recording of sex, but it is also an exemplary Schrader work, a painfully funny and misanthropic treatise on American masculinity and its sexualised image. (Williams 2003: 36)

> Paul Schrader's initially toothsome, finally sobering biopic casts Crane as another of its director's doomed narcissists – a man whose inability to focus on anything but himself sucks him into a fetid whirlpool of sleaze and alienation. Greg Kinnear is frighteningly plausible in the role. (Robey 2003)

Crane's family had issues with aspects of his portrayal. Scotty, Crane's son with his second wife, and *Hogan's Heroes* co-star Sigrid Valdis, wrote, '*Auto Focus* is a monument to everything rotten in so-called "biopics" today; it's based on nothing but rumour and innuendo and is not the true story of Bob Crane's life. Period. Not even close' (Crane 2002). He goes on to refute many of the film's claims: Crane was not a regular churchgoer; he had been photographing his sex acts from 1956 (and always with their consent); he did not engage in S&M; he did not have a penile implant or a vasectomy and he only met John Carpenter in 1975. He does, however, confirm that his mother knew about the extra marital relationships and the filming (ibid.).

Further viewing

The Audrey Hepburn Story (Steve Robmar, 2000); Jennifer Love Hewitt
    (Audrey Hepburn)
The Girl (Julian Jarrold, 2012); Alfred Hitchcock (Toby Jones)
Gods and Monsters (Bill Condon, 1998); James Whale (Ian McKellen)
Good Night, and Good Luck (George Clooney, 2005); Edward R. Morrow

(David Strathairn)

Hitchcock (Sacha Gervasi, 2012); Alfred Hitchcock (Anthony Hopkins)

Hollywoodland (Allen Coulter, 2006); George Reeves (Ben Affleck)

Hugo (Martin Scorsese, 2011); Ben Kingsley (Georges Méliès)

The Life and Death of Peter Sellers (Stephen Hopkins, 2004); Peter Sellers (Geoffrey Rush)

Lovelace (Rob Epstein and Jeffrey Friedman, 2013); Linda Lovelace (Amanda Seyfried)

My Week with Marilyn (Simon Curtis, 2011); Marilyn Monroe (Michelle Williams), Laurence Olivier (Kenneth Branagh)

The Notorious Bettie Page (Mary Harron, 2006); Bettie Page (Gretchen Mol)

Saving Mr Banks (John Lee Hancock, 2013); Tom Hanks (Walt Disney)

3   PRICK UP YOUR EARS: NOW A WORD ON WRITERS

Let us look at the writer. What do you see – only a person who sits with a pen in his hand in front of piece of paper? That tells us little or nothing?' – Virginia Woolf, *The Leaning Tower* (1940)

There is nothing more dull than filming someone writing. Yet there have been some great fiction films that have focused entirely on the writing process, including *Barton Fink* (1991) and *Adaptation* (2002). Although fictitious, both based their lead writers on real people: playwright Clifford Odets (Barton Fink in *Barton Fink*) and screenwriter Charlie Kaufman (Charlie and Donald Kaufman in *Adaptation*). When it comes to filming the lives of real writers, there has been a tendency to downplay the actual act of writing and focus instead on their private lives. Either drawing parallels between what they write about and their lives, or how events serve as inspiration for their emotional inner life and its transfer to the written page.

Of all the creative arts, writing is the one that directors often find difficult to convey on screen. Films featuring musicians allow for performances and instant public responses; the painter, the resulting canvas: for the sportsman we instantly see them win/lose; for those based on the lives of film directors/actors we can see recreations of their work. But what of the writer? How often have you seen the clichéd montage sequence of writing, screwing up paper into balls, cuts to overflowing waste paper basket full of failed attempts? *Shakespeare in Love* (1998) pastiches this familiar trope marvellously.

Here we will examine the lives of three writers, and four interpretations of their lives: Iris Murdoch in *Iris*, Harvey Pekar in *American Splendor* and two versions of Truman Capote in *Capote* and *Infamous*.

Iris (2001)

Director: Richard Eyre
Screenwriters: Richard Eyre and Charles Wood
Starring: Judi Dench (Iris Murdoch (old)), Kate Winslet (Iris Murdoch (young)), Jim Broadbent (John Bayley (old)), Hugh Bonneville (John Bayley (young)), Timothy West (Maurice (old)) and Simon West (Maurice (young))
Subject: Irish-born British novelist Iris Murdoch (Jean Iris Murdoch, 1919–99)

Screenwriters Richard Eyre and Charles Wood used John Bayley's 1998 and 1999 memoirs of his wife, Iris Murdoch (*Elegy for Iris*, *Iris: A Memoir* and *Iris and Her Friends*) as the source material for *Iris*. By using these first-hand accounts of Bayley's emotional relationship with Murdoch, the film offers a tender portrait of marriage and love, first, a writer's life, second.

Iris's publicity material announced: 'Miramax is proud to present a film about one of the most extraordinary women of her time. With two of the most acclaimed actresses of their time.' This statement makes no mention either of the film's subject or the two actresses playing her. Nor is there any mention of what made her 'extraordinary'. The poster image is striking black-and-white portraits of Judi Dench (in the foreground) and Kate Winslet (behind). Only half their faces are shown, making clear that these two actresses together make a whole.

Eschewing a chronological approach, with a young Murdoch (Winslet) segueing to an older (Dench), the film's structure offers two parallel time-lines and Eyre and Wood's screenplay interweaves the past and present (two narratives, fifty years apart). We see Bayley and Murdoch at Oxford in the 1930s/40s falling in love and their life together in the 1990s dealing with Murdoch's decline into Alzheimer's.

Her loss of memory, creating a sense of loss of one's self, is central. It is a film about relationships, and the impact illness has on it, not the ill-

Kate Winslet as young Iris Murdoch and Hugh Bonneville as young John Bayley in *Iris* (2001)

ness *per se*. It is a film about storytelling, not the act of writing. The portrait of intellect dimmed is played out alongside the earlier timeframe showing a young and vibrant Murdoch, clearly Bayley's intellectual superior. As a young man he cannot keep up with her. On a bicycle ride, Bayley desperately tries to catch up and hold on to Iris who tells him: 'Keep tight hold of me and it'll be alright.' This cuts to the older Murdoch, following him around, nudging him, forgetting things until he shouts out in despair, leaving her confused. This is a film about people loving one another, needing one another. The fact that it is about real people (and one who had reached such intellectual greatness) makes the film more complex and more emotionally devastating, encapsulated by Murdoch asking of Bayley, 'We all worry about going mad, don't we? How would be know? Those of us who live in our minds, anyway. Other people would tell us – wouldn't they?'

Eyre shows them young and alive, but having seen their final darker years makes these earlier happier times all the more powerful and heart-breaking because we know how their story will end. We know their future (which neither of the young couple do) and we in their present, know their past (which Murdoch is beginning to forget) – leaving Bayley, a literary critic and writer, as repository of both their memories and chronicler of their lives.

The film was praised for its emotional content, and for not shying away from its narrative drive in focusing on the emotional interrogation of relationships:

[the actors] deliver fearless performances and bring enormous warmth, vitality and messy humanity to people who, as Murdoch says in the film, largely 'live in our minds'. Dench and Broadbent tactfully evoke the abstracted nature of Iris and John's relationship … compassionately, often painfully, portray[ing] the slippage of oncoming disease. (Hornaday 2002)

Its critics railed against the decision to exorcise the years where Murdoch was achieving greatness in her professional field.

If you only knew female writers from recent trips to the cinema, you might be forgiven for imagining that mental illness came with the job. With an understandable sense of dramatic priorities, *Sylvia*, *The Hours* and *Iris* have all taken more or less as read the dull business of writing books, in order to get on with the Oscar-winning suffering, and the awful pangs of love (with male writers being the likely cause). (Caines 2004)

Richard Eyre commented that Judi Dench, 'brought to the film [an] incandescent goodness and decency' (quoted in Tucker 2001). This may account for Dench's success at major national awards. She has been nominated for seven acting Academy Awards, five of which were for real people, and fifteen film BAFTAs, nine for real people. For Bayley, 'Watching the film was not primarily an emotional experience, but an aesthetic one. "How well they have done us," I thought. Not how weird and even threatening it feels to see oneself and one's loved one walking and talking on film' (2002).

American Splendor (2003)

Director: Robert Pulcici and Shari Springer Berman
Screenwriters: Robert Pulcici and Shari Springer Berman
Starring: Paul Giamatti (Harvey Pekar) and Hope Davis (Joyce Brabner)
Subject: American underground comic book writer Harvey Pekar (Harvey Lawrence Pekar, 1939–2010)

Paul Giamatti stars as Harvey Pekar, who through a series of ironically titled comic book series in which he stars, became an underground cult figure and quasi-celebratory. Pekar's comic book series *American Splendor* and *Our Cancer Year,* which he wrote with his wife Joyce Brabner, provided the film's source material.

Pekar began writing in 1976, and published 31 issues plus two larger works including *Our Movie Year*, a collection of comics written (with Brabner) about or at the time of the film's production and its effect on them.

American Splendor was written and directed by husband-and-wife team Shari Springer Berman and Robert Pulcini, whose previous films had been documentaries. Here they blend fact and fiction to create an entirely different way of presenting a life story, one that befits the most unlikely of subjects: a gloomy hypochondriac hospital file clerk. At the time of filming, Pekar was in his sixties, and had spent his life in the rundown Midwest industrial town of Cleveland, Ohio, working until his recent retirement at a Federal Department of Veteran Affairs hospital. He is a grey man, a forgettable and nondescript character. He is unprepossessing and unappealing in manner, appearance and personal hygiene. An obsessive collector of records and comic books, well read and articulate but not great on cleanliness or social interaction. We know this, as he has detailed his everyday life in minute detail in his comic books that are pessimistic and unrelenting.

The film focuses on the unlikely love story between Pekar and Brabner, his cancer scare, and their adoption of a teenage girl. Not much happens in the comic book, or in the film. But it is the way the story is told and the observations from the sidelines of the real Pekar and Brabner that elevate this film. There is an unpredictability to it, as there is in the courtship. Shortly after she vomits in his lavatory on their first date, she says to him: 'Let's just cut the courtship and get married.'

Pekar did not read the script before filming started. How do we know? Because he stops mid-way reading the voice-over for something to drink, and in interview he tells the director. It is that kind of film. The first time he is reading the script (or purports to be) is for the movie itself. His comic books played with form, so does the movie, using comic book aesthetics, incorporating animated sequences and split screen. In the comic books, different artists drew Pekar in different ways. The directors' draw on these differing comic-strip representations, as Giamatti will frequently turn into a line-drawn comic version of himself. The screen is divided into boxes, thought and speech bubbles appear. Where there is temporal or location change, it is indicated in the top right hand corner of the screen.

Paul Giamatti as Harvey Pekar in *American Splendor* (2003)

For the majority of the film Paul Giamatti plays Pekar and Hope Davis plays his third wife, Joyce Brabner. Along the way we also meet the real Harvey Pekar, Joyce Brabner and a number of Pekar's colleagues who he introduces in the comic strip and therefore into the movie, most notably Toby Radloff.

The film's opening sequence sets up this collage approach with the off-screen Pekar commenting on the on-screen action of Giamatti as Pekar. Pekar's croaks his voice-over, 'here's our man', as we see Giamatti slouch across the screen, 'Yeah alright, here's me. Or the guy who plays me anyway. He doesn't even look like me,' he grumbles. The on-screen action then cuts to the real Pekar in a staged-studio recording the voice-over and chatting with Shari Springer Berman. The audience can then instantly compare the real and the performance, seeing how good Giamatti is at emulating Pekar's poor posture, depressed demeanour, and how good the costume and make-up department have captured the look. 'Who is the real Harvey Pekar? Who could be more real than Paul Giamatti with his shrewd comic timing and professional body language? Could the "real" Joyce and Harvey have played themselves with comparable conviction?' (French 2004).

Pekar's stories are grounded in realism and naturalism, and the film's cinematography reflects this by working in earthy tones and sourcing film stock to complement the grey and browns (no primary or bright colours) of the Cleveland landscape. The documentary sequences are filmed in a completely artificial environment, a painted white studio space with vibrant colours, playfully subverting the usual aesthetics of non-reality versus reality. Here, the 'documentary' sequences are as much a fantasy as the core 'fiction'.

The barrier breaks down and the real 'characters' cross the barrier to share a fictional space with their off-screen counterparts. The use of framing, so essential in the comic book, is broken through here. Pekar and Toby (Judah Friedlander) finish a scene and leave the frame, which is reveled to be a set. They walk to an 'off-set area' where the real Toby and Pekar are snacking at the food table discussing the various merits of coloured jellybeans. Another example creates is a curious hall-of-mirrors effect when we see Giamatti as Pekar leave a network studio's green-room to appear live on the *David Letterman Show*, while Davis as Brabner watches archive footage of the real Pekar on a television screen.

American Splendor was firmly conceived and marketed as an 'art house' movie. Independent in spirit, style, budget and distribution, it was successful on the film festival circuit, winning the first prize at Sundance. It was nominated for Best Adapted Screenplay at the Academy Awards but, although clearly a greater adaptation achievement, lost out in the Hollywood-machine to *Lord of the Rings: The Return of the King* (2003).

The dichotomy of mainstream/art house was raised by Joe Morgenstern:

> sometimes the question of which review gets displayed on the cover and which goes inside is less parochial – or arbitrary – than it may seem. This week it's a reflection of the movie industry's separate-and-unequal distribution structure. The conventional and exemplary *Open Range* is opening in more than 2,000 theaters across the country. *American Splendor* is wildly unconventional, sensationally funny and a brilliant achievement by any measure – it renews your faith in the vitality of the movie medium. But this independent feature is opening Friday in exactly five theaters across the US. (2003)

Excellent performances and a light-hearted tone helped to create positive reviews in both the UK and US:

By choosing a subject whose life and art are inextricable, they've made the rare artist biopic that goes beyond the dull march of events and actually illuminates the creative process. (Tobias 2003)

The film is very funny without resorting to condescension, but also genuinely touching in its desire to celebrate a man quite remarkable for being so very unremarkable. The killer strategy (crucial if the film is to avoid a charge of patronising caricature) is to have Pekar, his likewise neurotic wife and equally unglamorous pals pop up regularly on screen to comment on and be compared to their lightly fictionalised counterparts as played (brilliantly) by the likes of Giamatti and Davis. (Andrew 2006b)

Capote (2005)

Director: Bennett Miller
Screenwriter: Dan Futterman
Starring: Philip Seymour Hoffman (Truman Capote) and Catherine Keener
    (Harper Lee)

[and]

Infamous (2006)

Director: Douglas McGrath
Screenwriter: Douglas McGrath
Starring: Toby Jones (Truman Capote), Sandra Bullock (Harper Lee)
Subject: American author, screenwriter and playwright Truman Capote
    (Truman Streckfus Persons 1924–84)

Truman Capote himself appeared in two films, playing the central role of Lionel Twain in the spoof detective film *Murder by Death* (1976) and a cameo (as himself) in Woody Allen's *Annie Hall* (1977). But he was primarily known as a guest on 1970s and 1980s chat shows, in which he increasingly appeared as a caricature of himself. Toby Jones commented, 'I've watched hours of television chat shows where audiences squirm at his high-pitched voice, and wonder whether this man could possibly be for real' (quoted in Christopher 2006). Truman Capote, as a character, has also appeared in two other bio-pics, *The Audrey Hepburn Story* (2000) and *The Hoax* (2006) and in the 2009 American television series *Life on Mars*. In all three, he was played by Michael J. Burg. In a quirky twist of casting, Burg plays Tennessee Williams in *Capote*.

Released within a year of one another, *Capote* and *Infamous* cover the same period of Capote's life, the six years from 1959 to 1965 whilst Capote was writing *In Cold Blood*, a true-crime account (in the style of a novel) of the 1959 murder of the Clutter family. Capote went to the small town of Holcomb in Kansas with his friend Harper Lee to research and interview those involved, including Perry Smith and Dick Hickock who were accused of the murders.

The two films used different source materials that have resulted in differences to their aesthetics, narrative choices, character development and performances. *Capote* used Gerald Clarke's biography *Capote* (1988). Former *Time* magazine contributor Clarke's biography was admired for presenting facts in an entertaining and enlightening manner. *Infamous* drew on *Truman Capote: In Which Various Friends, Enemies, Acquaintances and Detractors Recall His Turbulent Career* (1998) by George Plimpton. It is presented as a sequence of quotes from interviews Plimpton conducted with more than 150 people who knew Capote. As *Infamous* was based on personal reminiscences of Capote by the people who knew him, this may account for its more affectionate portrayal.

In Cold Blood (1966) sold millions and achieved great critical acclaim, something that Capote was never able to replicate, increasingly appearing as merely a chat show guest before he died in a haze of pills and booze in 1984. Capote is not a character included *In Cold Blood* at all, although his very presence in Kansas for all those years affected the case. There have been considerable debates about how his involvement in the case may have affected its outcome as well as controversies that in the book he made up quotes and incidents that never happened.

The two films, although covering the same period, are very different in tone and style, and are full of contradictions. Perhaps contrasting their accuracy forms part of a greater understanding of the relationship between fact and fiction. Critics of Capote's 'non-fiction novel' have disagreed with him over his emphasis and handling of purported events. Capote used fictional methods to embellish – some say fabricate – his reporting of the

Philip Seymour Hoffman as Truman Capote and Catherine Keener as Harper Lee in *Capote* (2005)

Toby Jones as Truman Capote and Sandra Bullock as Harper Lee in *Infamous* (2006)

murders of the Clutter family. We may never know what actually occurred during many of the encounters between Capote, Smith and the others over that five-year period. Capote was never shy about creating myths to entertain his acolytes, predominantly New York society women, known as 'swans', who adored him. *Infamous* shows this side of him, with more of his New York life where we see him coax his 'swans' into sharing their secrets, which he later uses as gossip fodder. The 'swans' are played by Sigourney Weaver, Juliet Stevenson, Hope Davis and Isabella Rossellini.

Capote was released in its original language in the countries that usually dub, in order to preserve Hoffman's extraordinary vocal performance where he captures Capote's strange high-pitched fey voice. Hoffman's performance is austere and restrained, about which he said: 'I was terrified to start with, because you don't want to mimic him, you don't want to just do a stunt, because the story is the important thing, so I knew that if I served the story, the character would could alive. I knew that when you were watching it, you had to be moved by the story' (quoted in Colley 2006).

Capote is a film about the bond of trust built up between an interviewer and interviewee, and how this can be just an illusion. Capote became fascinated with Smith, and the film hints that he developed an infatuation with him. It implies that he deliberately supplied Smith and Hickock with inferior lawyers, as the only suitable ending for his book would be their death by execution. Once they hang, Capote says to Lee, 'I couldn't have done anything to save them', to which she responds, 'Maybe not, Truman. But the truth is you didn't want to.'

Infamous initially seems lighter and frothier, the scenes in New York are peppered with sparkly wit, and infused with biting black humour. When Capote goes to Kansas to meet Smith, it becomes much darker in tone. Whereas *Capote* hinted at the infatuation with Smith, in *Infamous* it is made more explicit. The erotic tensions between Capote (Jones) and Perry Smith (Daniel Craig) unmistakable. Craig said: 'There was never any self-consciousness about it. I always think that's how a love story needs to play out anyway, because it's just this friendship that starts growing, and if it turns into sex, it turns into sex; but it's not like two young men meet in a bar, go out back and fuck. This is about two human beings really sitting down and trying to figure each other out' (quoted in Hoggard 2006).

Infamous thus makes more explicit the homosexual bond between Capote and Perry. McGrath in the DVD commentary said, 'I couldn't even believe I wrote this [of Capote's near rape by Smith]. The scene was so alarming and upsetting to watch, even on set – my palms were sweating.' Capote is shown to be clearly enamoured of Smith, and his feelings are requited. He is clearly distressed when Smith is executed. *Capote* depicts the author as more manipulative, willing to say or do anything to get Smith to tell his story, even being shown withholding information.

On the subject of the two films, Craig commented: 'My feeling all the way along was I wish they had put the two bloody films out together. I wish they'd had the balls to do that. I love Truman Capote, and I love *In Cold Blood* so much, I thought, "You know what, whatever happens, this is worth telling. It's worth seeing another interpretation of that character"' (ibid.). Sigourney Weaver adds: 'If the other film [*Capote*] is like a shot of bourbon, then this is a glass of champagne' (ibid.).

Comparing the two, New Yorker Philip Seymour Hoffman offers a more nuanced, oblique performance, generated through a muted screenplay that avoids graphic scenes in favour of a subtler approach and a darker tone throughout.

A tragic obsession pervades Toby Jones's performance of Capote who offers a very different emotional performance than Hoffman's. Jones says:

How do you humanise a character who is utterly extreme. He comes across as such a freak: the mannerisms, the silly clothes and the compulsive name dropping of jet-set friends. The hardest challenge was creating a character that people might actually want to care about. The great comfort of a script as good as *Infamous* is that almost every word is brand new. There are previous few borrowed quotes, and every single situation is imagined. No one knows exactly what happened between Capote and Perry Smith in the prison cell during their meetings. That's really the whole point. (Quoted in Christopher 2006)

Adam Smith, in his tribute to Philip Seymour Hoffman following the great actor's untimely death, writes:

Hoffman's transformation into Truman Capote remains one of the great achievements of any recent film career. Capote was tiny, fey, and precise in his movements. Hoffman, superficially at least, could occasionally resemble a '70s wrestler on the decline [Hoffman was 5ft 9, Capote 5ft 3]. But, through a sheer act of creative will Hoffman metamorphosed seamlessly into the elfin wordsmith. The commitment to the transformation, to that strange, alien voice was total. An Oscar for the simple craft of acting has never been more deserved. (Smith 2014: 26)

Capote was released 30 September 2005, to coincide with Truman Capote's birthday. It opened to great critical acclaim, as was Hoffman's portrayal within award circles. *Infamous* premiered at the Venice film festival in August 2006.

Most of the critical discussions focused on comparisons to the earlier film.

Both actors offer convincing voice and style impersonations. Shawn Levy describes Hoffman's as 'note-perfect. The wheezy laugh, the pain of work, the prying nature, the cold eye, the self-obsession, the ability to perform and ingratiate and wheedle – it's Capote you're watching up there' (2005) and Peter Bradshaw points out that 'British actor Toby Jones plays Capote and certainly looks the part – more so than Hoffman. It's a very good performance and Jones deserves his time in the spotlight' (2007a). And A. O. Scott of the New York Times wrote:

> Mr. Jones's impersonation is touching and credible, and his notion of the character is interestingly different from that of Philip Seymour Hoffman, star of *Capote*. In general, *Infamous* is warmer and more tender … less a parable of literary ethics than a showcase of literary personality, and it is in the end more touching than troubling. The release of two movies on the same subject is somewhat unusual, and the arrival in close succession of two good movies that tell more or less identical stories, each one distinguished by real intelligence in conception and execution, is downright uncanny. (2006)

Further viewing

Becoming Jane (Julian Jarrold, 2007); Jane Austen (Anne Hathaway)
Bright Star (Jane Campion, 2009); John Keats (Ben Wishaw) and Fanny Brawne (Abbie Cornish)
The Diving Bell and the Butterfly (Julian Schnabel, 2007); Jean-Dominique Bauby (Mathieu Almaric)
The Edge of Love (John Maybury, 2008); Dylan Thomas (Matthew Rhys)
The Hours (Stephen Daldry, 2002); Nicole Kidman (Virginia Woolf)
Howl (Rob Epstein and Jeffrey Friedman, 2010); Allen Ginsberg (James Franco)
Kill Your Darlings (John Krokidas, 2013); Allen Ginsberg (Daniel Radcliffe), Jack Kerouac (Jack Houston) and William Burroughs (Ben Foster)
The Last Station (Michael Hoffman, 2009); Leonard Tolstoy (Christopher Plummer)

Miss Austen Regrets (Jeremy Lovering, 2007); Jane Austen (Olivia Williams)

Miss Potter (Chris Noonan, 2006); Renee Zellweger (Beatrix Potter)

Mrs. Parker and the Vicious Circle (Alan Rudolph, 1994); Dorothy Parker (Jennifer Jason Leigh)

Saving Mr Banks (John Lee Hancock, 2013); P. L. Travers (Emma Thompson)

Sylvia (Christine Jeffs, 2003); Sylvia Plath (Gwyneth Paltrow) and Ted Hughes (Daniel Craig)

Wilde (Brian Gilbert, 1998); Oscar Wilde (Stephen Fry)

4   THROUGH THE EYES OF A PAINTER: THE ART OF THE ON-SCREEN ARTIST

The lives of great artists, in fact, tend to make irresistible cinema because of their very affinities with melodrama and myth – most of them possessing 'the whole kit' as Tom Wolfe might say, of a classical, five-act tragedy.

        – Michael Bracewell, *Sight and Sound* (June 2002)

As with writers, the lives of artists depicted on film imply that if you are creatively blessed then you will also be emotionally scarred. Many times, filmmakers fail to balance the art with the life. The two films discussed here come closer than many at exploring and making cinematic the actual act of painting itself.

    The two case studies chosen explore the lives of two painters Frida Kahlo (Salma Hayek) and Jackson Pollock (Ed Harris). They were deeply personal projects for their stars, who also produced and worked closely on the screenplay; Harris also directed. Both place the exploration and depiction of their craft in parallel with the emotional turmoil of their lives.

Pollock (2000)

Director: Ed Harris
Screenwriters: Barbara Turner and Susan J. Emshwiller
Starring: Ed Harris (Jackson Pollock) and Marcia Gay Harden (Lee Krasner)
Subject: American painter Jackson Pollock (Paul Jackson Pollock 1912–56)

Ed Harris as Jackson Pollock in *Pollock* (2000)

In the late 1980s Ed Harris's father, noticing a physical resemblance between his son and the painter Jackson Pollock, gave Harris a biography of the artist, *Jackson Pollock: An American Saga* (1989) by Stephen Naifeh and Gregory White Smith, which was used as the source material.

Over the next fifteen years Harris's interest became a desire to bring Pollock's complex life to the screen. Whilst developing a strong reputation as an actor, he continued to work on this project, and began to study and emulate Pollock's free-forming drip-style painting techniques so that he could authentically recreate them in the film. He then worked with screenwriters Barbara Turner and Susan J. Emshwiller to bring the artist's life to the screen and find financing. It was Harris's first film as director.

Having convinced the Pollock–Krasner Foundation that he was not interested in exploiting Pollock and Krasner (his wife), they gave their full support. The sequences in Long Island were filmed in their actual house which is now the Pollock–Krasner Museum and Study Center. They granted him permission to use images of Pollock's paintings, and he commissioned three painters to make faithful replicas for use in the film (the lead artist was Lisa Lawley).

This has not always been possible; permission was not given for *Surviving Picasso* (James Ivory, 1996) and *Basquiat* (Julian Schnabel, 1996) where the works featured were 'in the style of...', and in *Love is the Devil* focusing on Francis Bacon, no completed works are shown.

The film was shot chronologically, and mid-way through filming Harris took a break of six weeks to gain 30lbs for the painter's final broken years, in the 1950s.

The film opens in the early 1950s when Pollock is at the height of his celebrity with people rushing (in slow motion) and thrusting copies of *Life* magazine at him for his signature. He is like a deer caught in the headlights; this fragile man is suddenly on the world stage and unable to cope. It then travels back to 1941 with Pollock as a penniless artist struggling to make a living in Greenwich Village. Lee Krasner, another artist influenced by the surrealist movement, strikes up a friendship which soon becomes romantic although rather dominating. Krasner is shown as a controlling influence; she begins to live for him and through him.

In 1943 he gets his first patron in Peggy Guggenheim (played by Harris's real wife Amy Madigan) who hosts a show for him and commissions a mural. By 1945 Pollock and Lee, now married, moved to a small town on Long Island. In 1947 he begins working on his large-canvas action paintings (aka the drip paintings) and becomes a success. *Life* magazine turns him into a star. The narrative has now returned to the film's opening scene. However, plagued by mental health and excessive drinking throughout his life, his relationship with Krasner becomes more and more strained, and his fame begins to adversey affect his work. By the mid-1950s he is having an affair with a young woman. She and a friend, Edith, are with the drunk Pollock when he crashes his car in 1956; both Pollock and Edith die in the incident.

The final few years of his life are rather skated over, offering no real sense of the deep abyss he was in. There were accusations that his work was getting progressively generic and those that had previous hailed him as American's greatest living artist were beginning to lose faith in him.

Harris has stated:

It was all-consuming. It was non-stop. It was very exhilarating. It was also very demanding and exhausting, but I didn't want anyone else to direct the film. I had worked on it long and hard and felt very intimate with it. In terms of playing Pollock, I just had been living with the guy and the thought of it for so long that I would just do it. We'd rehearse and stuff, but it was weird. Because, I'd shift. I'd act and then I'd go back behind a camera and check what we did. But I

was able to separate my mind a bit so when I was playing Pollock, I
was pretty much just in there. Sometimes I'd carry it a little bit over
into the directing aspect of things. I might lose my temper a little
bit or get a little abrasive or something. Because I was in character
somewhat, but most people understood that was part of the deal.
(Quoted in Kleinman 2003)

The film offers no flashbacks, there is no back story, no explanation as to
how Pollock became the way he was, as there is in *Ray*. Early scripts did
include flashbacks to his childhood as a way of explaining his later behaviour, but these were pulled because of budget constraints. Also, Harris has
stated: 'I never wanted to make it a psychoanalytic kind of trip. First of
all, you can conjecture, you can guess what he was like in his youth growing up, but he was also just born differently. It's like I don't want to try to
explain that' (quoted in Cheng 2001). It was believed that he was a manic
depressive and used alcohol as a prop, throughout the period covered in
the film (1940–56), from his first meeting with Krasner to his death.

As Harris had been painting for ten years in the style of Pollock his performance lacks inhibition and has the intensity one would associate with
Pollock. Having been commissioned to paint his first large-scale mural, in a
montage scene the film sees him pacing, sitting staring at this huge canvas
dominating his small apartment. It fills the screen – looming large, then in
a frenzy of activity he begins to work. Harris had deftly choreographed the
painting as though it was a dance. The fluid moments, mirroring the brush-
strokes, creating the painting in front of us. 'The idea was not to imperson-
ate him, not to try to recreate anything specifically; but just to try to paint,
in the moment, in his style' (Harris quoted in Matheou 2002).

Pollock grossed just over $10.5 million at the international box office,
the vast majority ($8.5 million) in the US. Both Harris and Gay Harden were
nominated for Academy Awards, she winning Best Supporting Actress.
Harris lost out to Russell Crowe in *Gladiator*. The film was also widely criti-
call praised:

The result is a quietly excellent movie, clearly a labour of love for
Harris, and far superior to much of the current Hollywood product.
It is aimed at educated adults. Daringly, almost experimentally,
Harris repudiates the classic three-act drama template, with its

explicit psychology and love-interest clichés, preferring to present Pollock's troubled career in a more indirect, interior way. He shows us detailed, revealing scenes from a life, sometimes entirely wordless, photographed and acted with unhurried intricacy and care. (Bradshaw 2002)

Frida (2002)

Director: Julie Taymor
Screenwriters: Clancy Sigal, Diane Lake, Gregory Nava, Anna Thomas, Rodrigo Garcia and Edward Norton
Starring: Salma Hayek (Frida Kahlo) and Alfred Molina (Diego Rivera)
Subject: Mexican painter Frida Kahlo (Magdalena Carmen Frieda Kahlo y Calderón, 1907–1954)

This was a personal project for Salma Hayek who nurtured the film as producer. Working from *Frida: A Biography of Frida Kahlo* by Hayden Herrera (2002), the film covers Kahlo's life from her near-fatal accident aged 16 to her death aged 47, played by Hayek throughout.

It details her development as an artist, hand-in-hand with her problematic marriage to Mexican mural painter Diego Rivera (Alfred Molina), her communist politics and her ill-health. It was directed by theatre and film director Julie Taymor, who observed 'Most movies about artists wallow in the angst, and they repel me' (quoted in Bosley 2002).

For Hayek it was a project that she had been nurturing for six years, first approaching Molina to co-star in 1998, fearful that other Hollywood actresses, including Madonna and Jennifer Lopez, were also developing projects. She secured the rights to use Kahlo's art from Dolores Olmedo Patino, a former lover and patron of Rivera who administers the rights to much of the couple's work. Rivera's grandchildren were also involved and were on set to ensure historical accuracy. Even the dogs used were descendants of Kahlo's dogs!

An original script by Gregory Nava was rewritten by Rodrigo Garcia (son of Gabriel García Márquez), and later re-worked when Walter Salles came on board to direct. He then left the project and Julie Taymor was signed-up, and she, Hayek, and her then boyfriend actor Edward Norton rewrote the script again. This version brought out more of the love story, and the politics. For Molina, 'I think [Norton] was very interested in the political dimension of these two people. He wanted to bring in the fact that they weren't just hugely talented artists, but also at the forefront of Mexican politics and progressive thinking' (quoted in Tuckman 2001). However, due to a Writer's Guild of America decision his name was not officially credited. Norton said, 'I got shafted by the Writer's Guild at the last minute, but I wrote the draft that got made' (quoted by Fischer 2002).

Frida was filmed over twelve weeks in the spring of 2001. Its locations included sites in Mexico City and the outlying towns of Puebla and San Luis Potosi. Locals lent period costumes and props to the production. Taymor and cinematographer Rodrigo Prieto worked to ensure that the cinematography, colour, use of light and composition mirrored Kahlo's paintings. Prieto said, 'We wanted to see Frida's world through her eyes, while still staying true to realistic settings and lighting designs. We took a lot of visual cues from her own letters and diaries; she wrote a lot about color and the "mystery of darkness"' (quoted in Bosley 2002).

The film opens in 1953, at Kahlo's first one-woman show in Mexico. Her doctor tells her she is too sick to attend, but she has her bed lifted into a flat-bed truck and carried to the gallery. Rivera's narration recalls the first time they met. 'There was this skinny kid with one eyebrow shouting up at my studio. She was an artist who tore open her chest and heart to reveal the biological truth of her feelings.' The film then flashes back to 1923, with Kahlo aged 16, young and full of hope. It then continues in a linear fashion, up to her tragic death at aged 47.

Kahlo was left semi-invalided after the tram accident and during her recuperation she began to paint. She pours the near-destruction and failures of her body on to the canvas. Her work explored the pain in her life: pain caused by the accident, miscarriages and her marriage, his and her affairs, divorce and remarriage. This pain shown in her work is manifestly evident on screen. Taymor said:

> When I read Herrera's book, I could really understand where the paintings came from in her life, which makes her very different from an abstract painter like Pollock or Picasso, with whom that's not so clear. Like many people, I found her paintings frighteningly gruesome and revealing, but as a film director, they appealed to me because of their narrative content. I thought that using pho-

Salma Hayek as Frida Kahlo in *Frida* (2002)

tography and visual effects to make them unfold before your eyes would be a great addition to what might otherwise be a normal biopic. (Quoted in Bosley 2002)

This is a film about an artist at work. Kahlo's work literally comes to life, through a mix of cinematography, digital effects and animation. Hayek would have the make-up, hair and costumes as depicted in the paintings, the live-action image then dissolving to correspond with the paintings ('The Two Fridas', 'Self Portrait With Cropped Hair' and 'The Broken Column'), or vice versa. Other paintings, such as 'My Dress Hangs There', 'The Suicide of Dorothy Hale' and 'What the Water Gave Me' were animated, retaining Kahlo's naïve style. When Kahlo and Rivera went to New York, she created magnificent montages of her time there and the sequence is filmed in a style of a montage incorporating live-action footage of the actors, cut-outs of the city skyline, postcards and period footage of the Detroit factory that Rivera actually toured. Taymor said, 'In the original script, Frida and Diego just walk down Fifth Avenue, and how boring can that be? Both Frida and Diego did montages in their paintings, so I wanted to do something in their style. That kind of agitprop photomontage is also true to that period. It was also a cheap way of creating a vast landscape' (ibid.).

The film also features an animated 'The Day of the Dead' sequence by the Quay Brothers. Following her tram accident, Kahlo is delirious, hearing her doctors discuss her diagnosis and she hallucinates that they are skeletons. Taymor says, 'I simply gave them a scenario; I said it was a nightmare featuring skeletons in the Mexican Day of the Dead style, and I stressed to make it abstract, comic but slightly frightening. I sent them books of woodcut artist [José Guadalupe] Posada and photos of the hospital room, and they ran with it' (ibid.). This placing of Kahlo's art so centrally lends a visually striking tone to what is otherwise a straightforward linear narrative telling of her life.

Hayek is on screen throughout and via a series of vignettes it becomes increasingly a film about her work and Rivera and less about the others that surround her. When it tries introducing her other lovers and relationships there is little time and it seems perfunctory and lacking emotional engagement. Alexander Walker noted that 'protagonists seem to have next to no small talk, but are always discussing the great events of their own lives or times. The attempt to introduce intimacy into the meeting of celebrities – "Leon, tell me about your children," says Frida, cuddling up to Trotsky's goatee – invites easy mockery' (2002).

The film's budget was $12 million, and it took $56 million on its worldwide cinema release. It was nominated for 47 awards across the season, picking up 17, but the critical reception was mixed:

> Long in gestation, the Frida Kahlo biopic, produced by and starring Salma Hayek, finally reaches our screens, bearing with it an Oscar nomination for best actress. Was it worth the wait? Well, it's pretty stodgy stuff, by and large, that covers all the expected bases, distilling Kahlo's relatively short, incident-packed life into the conventional parameters of the artist biography – lots of wine-drinking, dramatic gestures and arguments about communism. Director Julie Taymor takes considerable pains over small, animated interpolations that briefly illustrate and draw on Kahlo's own work; however impressive these are, though, they're not enough to offset the heaviness of the rest of the film. Kahlo's iconic value – both as a poster girl for 1980s western bohemianism and for Mexico's own sense of pride – is well established, and the movie doesn't let them down. (Pulver 2003)

Further viewing

Basquiat (Julian Schnabel, 1996); Jean-Michel Basquiat (Jeffrey Wright)
Fur: An Imaginary Portrait of Diane Arbus (Steven Shainberg, 2006); Diane
    Arbus (Nicole Kidman)
Goya's Ghosts (Milos Forman, 2006); Francisco de Goya (Stellan Skars-
    gaard)
Klimt (Raoul Ruiz, 2006); Gustav Klimt (John Malkovich)
Love is the Devil (John Maybury, 1998); Francis Bacon (Derek Jacobi)
Paradise Found (Mario Andreacchio, 2003); Paul Gauguin (Kiefer
    Sutherland)
Surviving Picasso (James Ivory, 1996); Pablo Picasso (Anthony Hopkins)

5   A WINNER NEVER QUITS: THE POWERFUL FORCE
OF SPORTING BIOGRAPHIES

The best sport films have as little to do with sport as possible. The
telling scenes in *Raging Bull* are not Robert de Niro as a champion
boxer but as a wife-beater and bloated has-been. *Chariots of Fire*
is not about running but loyalty to country, to one's religious faith
and to social class.
                      – Matt Dickinson, *The Times* (19 March 2009)

Following on from Dickinson's observation above, the more successful
sports bio-pics seem to be those where the sporting figure has challenged
the system, or overcome great adversity to become the legends they are.
Narratives driven on the premise that the underdog can succeed have
always proved a popular draw at the box office.

The two case studies here, *Ali* and *The Damned United* (2009), show
two sports (boxing and football) from two countries (US and UK) from an
overlapping period of the late 1960s to early 1970s. Both films have at
their core a significant sporting incident in 1974. *The Damned United* features archive footage of Muhammad Ali playfully addressing a message
to Clough: 'Some fella in London, England named, some Brian ... Brian
Clough. I heard all the way in America that this fella talks too much. They
say he's another Muhammed Ali. There's just one Muhammed Ali. Now,

Clough, I've had enough. Stop it.' They continued their friendly rivalry as to who is the biggest 'talker' over the years, meeting twice.

Ali (2001)

Director: Michael Mann
Screenwriters: Stephen J. Rivele, Christopher Wilkinson, Michael Mann
    and Eric Roth
Starring: Will Smith (Muhammad Ali)
Subject: American boxer Muhammed Ali (Cassius Marcellus Clay, jr 1942
    – present)

'Forget what you think you know', promised the film's teaser trailer. At its heart *Ali* depicts the ten-year period from 1964 to 1974. There are occasional flashbacks to his childhood, particularly with reference to segregation, showing him being told to get to the back of the bus.

This ambitious project was a decade in the making. Screenwriter Stephen J. Rivele said:

> The big challenge in *Ali* was reducing this enormous life to a manageable size. That means selecting the events that we wanted to dramatize and creating a structure in which we could portray those events. It was a huge task of selecting the specific events we wanted to focus on in order to create a portrayal of the man that would speak to an audience today ... scenes that would illuminate the inner life of the characters and dramatize his spiritual quest, because to us the film was about a man starting to learn the will of God for himself and seeking to do the will of God. (Quoted in Coppola 2002: 16)

The original script by Rivele and Christopher Wilkinson covered the period from 1960 to the present day. Michael Mann (with Eric Roth) re-worked it, reducing the time period to 1964–74, and focusing on his career and religious transformation. Mann was less interested in Ali's spiritual journey but more in his sociological significance.

Smith and Mann both deferred their salaries against cost overruns to ensure that they were able to film the Zaire sequences in Africa. The film's budget was $100 million; Smith and Mann agreed to pay for any additional over-spends out of their own pocket. Mann said, 'We were very committed to this [project]. You're looking at two guys that have put some material stuff where their mouth is' (Cooney Carrillo 2001: 47).

Will Smith trained extensively for the role and spent a year learning to box: 'I was hit and it hurt … in boxing movies every punch is dead on whereas in a real fight you see guys fight six, seven rounds before some- body gets a clean shot' (Cooney & Palmer 2002: 38). Smith was consid- ered a brave choice as at the time he had a reputation for witty comedy/ light action, but he took the job seriously, and worked hard to achieve a boxer's physique and dynamism; he was 195lbs and went up to 223lbs (with muscle). Mann said, 'You can't imitate Ali, you gotta be him, so you gotta be prepared to go all the way. Will did that by preparing for a year, so that he'd naturally fight, speak and move like Ali' (Andrew 2002).

Smith was first approached to make the movie in 1995:

Sure I was hesitant. From my own standpoint, I knew I would never play Muhammad Ali. It was just too gargantuan a task and the margin of error was entirely too small. I just refused to be that guy that messed up this story. For years, I turned it down. Officially, five times and unofficially? Probably 34 or 35 times. It was only when I met Michael Mann two years ago that I could see how it could be done. (Quoted in Goldman 2002)

Ali was involved in the making of the film, and endorsed it, which perhaps explains Mann's respectful approach. What the film suffers from is the filmmakers' reverence for Ali the legend – not the man. Ali, still alive and suffering from Parkinson's Disease, is a mere shadow of the man at the peak of his career that demanded such loyalty and passion. The filmmakers tread carefully, perhaps too carefully. Most affecting are the scenes where Ali is walking the streets, unable to do anything without being mobbed by fans and well-wishers. However, the film turns his loud and proud into wise and statesmanlike so that he becomes dull. The funniest scenes are those with sports presenter, friend and mentor Howard Cossell (Jon Voight).

[Ali came to the set] one time I went 'that's it, I'm fighting you right now sucker! I'm whipping you right now!' I'm ranting and raving,

Ali (2002)

throwing chairs all over and at the end of 15 minutes Ali turned to
his long-time friend Howard Cossell and said 'Man, how come you
didn't tell me I was so crazy?' (Smith quoted in Cooney & Palmer
2002: 39)

The cinematography moves between colour and sepia. The first half of the
film shows his boxing matches alongside the social milieu and his alle-
giance to the Black Muslims, the racial politics, his refusal to be drafted
and the subsequent legal battles which demonstrate a man in control both
in the ring and out of it. The second half of the film sees a shift from the
sport and politics to the personal effect these have on this marriages.

The boxing matches are brutally realistic and careful replicas of their
originals. As Smith noted, 'It felt like preparing for three different films at
once. The boxing was a year's worth of work ... work[ing] to get the synco-
pation of his voice was a whole other training. Then the dialect, the mannerisms, then understanding the man' (Cooney & Palmer 2002: 39).

The film opens before Ali's championship debut against Sonny Liston
(Michael Bentt), where you see both his verbal and physical prowess.
This match would have been less well-known to cinema audiences than
the later 'Rumble in the Jungle', where Smith and Charles Shufford are
mere shadows of Ali and Foreman. The original would have been fresh in
people's minds at the time of this film's original release, as it had been
the subject of the documentary feature *When We Were Kings* (Leon Gast,
1996). The fifteen-round battle with Joe Frazier at Madison Square Gardens

is reduced to its closing moments. There is no exploration of the effect this public knockout had for Ali; it serves merely as prologue for the comeback trail sequence which follows.

The film was sold on the realism of the boxing bouts. All of the other boxers in the films ware former heavyweight boxers. They were keen to avoid Hollywood-style boxing of the early *Rocky* films which featured shots mostly hitting the air, or Stallone moving around with no defence whatsoever, nor did they want to emulate the hyper-stylised techniques of *Raging Bull* (Martin Scorsese, 1980). The spinning camera in the fight sequences aids the audience in feeling the boxer's disorientation and is as powerful as anything in Scorsese's film, but they serve only to highlight the scenes outside of the ring, which remain static. We are shown what Ali's life was like, but not why.

It is in the verbal pre-match sparring where Ali comes to life and we see Ali the performer. Also these are the moments where Smith is most like his popular on-screen persona. We see precious little of Ali the man; the film does not dwell on some of the more problematic aspects of his life – the mistreatment of his wives, neglect of his children, his refusal to serve his country in Vietnam. His political and religious stances are overshadowed or confusing.

Ali was an entertainer, a clown – but he is shown as pensive and saint-like. He went beyond the mere role of boxer within his lifetime to that of an icon. Yet *Ali* does not convey the charm and charisma of the man himself, as seen in documentaries *Muhammad Ali: The Greatest* (William Klein, 1974) or *When We Were Kings* or indeed the flawed bio-pic *The Greatest* (Tom Gries, 1977) in which Ali starred as himself.

Reviewers tended to focus on Smith's performance and his obvious commitment to the role. The spirit of Ali is lacking in *Ali,* doing little to serve as a tribute the man. It engages but does not inspire.

Mann's overwhelming love of his subject will turn audiences into exuberant, thrilled fight crowds. Smith captures Ali's musicality, pausing in midsyllable while ranting and exhaling to punch things up and turn even a joke into something operatic. We see the movie levitate when Ali and Brown chant, 'Float like a butterfly,' the slogan that takes on a different meaning in each context, starting off as hopeful and spry, finally becoming rueful and pointed. When the film pulls off moments like these, it's breathtaking — a near great movie. (Mitchell 2001)

Ali is a long, flat, curiously muted film about the heavyweight champion. It lacks much of the flash, fire and humor of Muhammad Ali and is shot more in the tone of a eulogy than a celebration. There is little joy here. The film is long and plays longer, because it permits itself sequences that are drawn out to inexplicable lengths while hurrying past others that should have been dramatic high points. (Ebert 2001)

Audiences stayed away, and the film lost an estimated $63 million at the box office on its original release. Mann would later revise it for the Director's Cut DVD release removing some material, and adding previously unseen footage.

The Damned United (2009)

Director: Tom Hooper
Screenwriter: Peter Morgan
Starring: Michael Sheen (Brian Clough), Timothy Spall (Peter Taylor), Colm
    Meaney (Don Revie) and Jim Broadbent (Sam Longson)
Subject: English footballer and football manager Brian Clough (Brian
    Howard Clough, 1935–2004)

Taking David Peace's fictionalised account of Brain Clough's 44-day tenure as manager of Leeds United, *The Damned Utd* (2006) as its basis, Peter Morgan's screenplay for *The Damned United* focuses on the friendship between Clough and Peter Taylor whilst at Derby Country, and Clough's rivalry with Leeds United manager Don Revie.

Hugh McIlvanney, 'The Voice of Sport', said of Peace's source novel:

Writers of fiction have an automatic license to play God but writers of faction seem to me to be in a different category, particularly when attributing motives and behaviour to the living. Peace and his publishers, Faber & Faber, have already been forced to respect such a distinction by the legal action they faced from John Giles [the

Leeds midfielder] ... He took formal exception to being depicted in the novel as a treacherous, relentlessly nasty plotter against the new manager. Faber & Faber made no admission of liability but paid a settlement to Giles and agreed to make changes to the text in subsequent editions.

Stephen Frears had sent the book to Morgan as a possible follow-up project after their success together on *The Deal* (2003) and *The Queen* (2006).

Peter Morgan has built a considerable reputation as a creator of bio-pics for film and television (and theatre, with *The Audience*, 2013) focusing on a single incident or moment in a person's life as a way of gaining insight into their life as whole: *The Deal, The Queen, Longford* (Tom Hooper, 2006), *The Last King of Scotland* (Kevin MacDonald, 2008), *Frost/Nixon* (Ron Howard, 2008), *The Special Relationship* (Richard Loncraine, 2010) and *Rush* (Ron Howard, 2013). In the US trailer for the film, it is his name as the man behind *The Queen* and *Frost/Nixon* that appears first.

His approach has proved a popular template, but has had its critics, wondering how factually accurate his versions are and how much of his representations of what may have happened are a fusion of fact and fiction. Morgan has said:

People are right to question that. They watch a film that is made with real characters, the message is 'We're hoping you believe it'. You may feel betrayed that stuff has been made up, but that's what makes it exciting. People should question what history is, and in whose hands it has been written. One person's history is another person's fiction. (Quoted in Teeman 2009)

Production was scheduled for 2007 with Frears directing, but he pulled out, and Morgan's *Longford* director Tom Hooper stepped in.

The film stars Michael Sheen, for whom this was his fifth collaboration with Peter Morgan. Sheen has garnered a similar reputation for real-life on-screen creations: Tony Blair (*The Deal, The Queen* and *The Special Relationship*), David Frost (*Frost/Nixon*), Kenneth Williams (*Fantabulosa!*, 2006), H.G. Wells (*H.G. Wells: War with the World*, 2006), Mark Furness (*Dirty Filthy Love*, 2004) and Bill Masters (*Masters of Sex*, TV 2013 – present). Sheen had been the first choice for Clough from the outset.

Michael Sheen as Brian Clough in *The Damned United* (2009)

Leo Robson in the *Times Literary Supplement* noted:

As Clough, Michael Sheen does another of his freaky body-snatches. One of the two central challenges here is Clough's Middlesbrough drawl [and] the other is catching Clough's easy way of self-aggrandisement. ... Here, Sheen does more than is required, delivering not just a deft impersonation but a limber performance, full of entertaining mischief; when he cracks his toothy grin, he looks like the Cheshire cat that got the cream. (2009)

The film's flashback structure effectively fills in the back story and history of the events of his time as manager of Derby County (with Taylor at his side) and his growing antagonism with Leeds manager Revie from 1968 to 1972, that brought him to the present-day storyline in 1974, when for 44 days Clough achieved his ambition of being the manager of Leeds United when Revie became England manager. His short tenure there was marred by long-held grudges and misgivings about the Leeds players reputation for violent and physical playing.

Most of the sporting action happens off-screen. During one crucial match, Clough stays in the dressing rooms. The suspense of the game generated from sound effects of the crowd to guide him of his team's progress.

The winning or losing of individual games is less important than the relationships Clough has with Taylor, Revie and Derby County owner

Longson, the film's focus being on men who let power and success go to their heads, and about the unbreakable bond between two friends. The Taylor/Clough relationship is played out more like a marriage, 'I bloody love you' as they embrace.

The trailer for the film was first shown on television prior to the kick-off of the FA Cup fourth round tie between Derby County and Nottingham Forest (both teams Clough managed) on 23 January 2009. The film was well-received by critics, but made less than its estimated $10 million budget at the box office, where it took slightly more than $4 million world-wide. It took less than $500,000 in the US where football (or 'soccer' as used in the trailer) and Brian Cough would have meant little.

Clough's widow Barbara and son Nigel were not involved in the film, as they had already expressed their dislike for the way Clough was portrayed in the novel. They felt the book represented a false picture of Clough, par-ticularly the portrayal of excessive swearing, smoking and drinking.Morgan did say, 'We tried so hard to involve the Clough family. We reached out, made offers. … We would so like their collaboration, but they've chosen not to, my conscience is clear' (quoted in Dawson 2009).

As a rebuttal to the book (and film), the Clough family collaborated with ITV for a seventy-minute documentary, *Clough* (2009), which was broadcast a week before the film's release. Within the programme Clough's friends and family variously described Peace's novel as 'dreadful', 'mean', 'wrong' and 'an outrageous betrayal'. John Giles, who had pursued Peace and Faber & Faber legally, pointed out that he was able 'to go to law [but there] were others [Billy Bremner, Don Revie and Clough himself] who were no longer able to defend their reputations' (quoted in McIlvanney 2009).

Further viewing

42 (Brian Helgeland, 2013); Jackie Robinson (Chadwick Boseman)
Amelia (Mira Nair, 2009); Amelia Earhart (Hilary Swank)
Cinderella Man (Ron Howard, 2005); James J. Braddock (Russell Crowe)
The Fighter (David O'Russell, 2010); Micky Ward (Mark Wahlberg) and
    Dickie Eklund (Christian Bale)
The Hurricane (Norman Jewison, 1999); Rubin 'Hurricane' Carter (Denzil
    Washington)
Moneyball (Bennett Miller, 2011); Billy Beane (Brad Pitt)

Rush (Ron Howard, 2013); James Hunt (Chris Hemsworth) and Nikki Lauda (Daniel Bruhl)

Seabiscuit (Gary Ross, 2003); Red Pollard (Toby Maguire)

Soul Surfer (Sean McNamara, 2011); Bethany Hamilton (AnnaSophia Robb)

6 AWAKENINGS: VOICES FROM THE IVORY TOWERS OF ACADEMIA

Contrary to conventional wisdom that entertainment media portray science and scientists in a negative light, research shows that across time, genre, and medium there is no single prevailing image and that both positive and negative images of scientists and science can be found. More recent research even suggests that in contemporary entertainment media, scientists are portrayed in an almost exclusively positive light and often as heroes.
– Matthew C. Nisbet, www.scienceblogs.com, 5 May 2010

Scientists, academics and technologists depicted from the 1930s to the 1950s were portrayed as 'heroes' working to make the world a safer, better place: One free from disease (*The Story of Louis Pasteur*, 1936) or tyranny (*The Dam Busters*, 1954). These were largely propaganda films meant to inspire audiences during a period of economic depression, the war and its aftermath.

In most recent years, such films have tended to offer a warts-and-all depiction, interweaving the academic prowess of their subjects with complex emotional stories. Both Kinsey in *Kinsey* and Nash in *A Beautiful Mind* are portrayed as flawed, but brilliant, men.

The two films selected here examine men working in academia during the same period. One, whose name became part of the public vocabulary within weeks of a revolutionary publication, Kinsey, the other, Nash, remained comparatively unknown until the film version of his life was released.

A Beautiful Mind (2001)

Director: Ron Howard
Screenwriter: Akiva Goldsman
Starring: Russell Crowe (John Nash), Jennifer Connelly (Alicia Nash) and
    Paul Bettany (Charles)
Subject: American mathematician John Nash (John Forbes Nash, Jr,
    1928–present)

Inspired by Sylvia Nasar's Pulitzer Prize-winning biography *A Beautiful Mind* (1998) which is academic in tone, Goldsman's screenplay echoes the themes but creates tensions by drawing out John Nash's paranoid obsessions and mental breakdown. His schizophrenia is not treated as a quirky character trait or as crippling tragedy; Nash is seen dealing with this illness and to an extent overcoming it.

Producer Brian Grazer optioned the book after reading an excerpt in *Vanity Fair* magazine. Goldsman was selected as screenwriter and when Ron Howard came on board as director, he sought additional script changes to emphasise the love story between Nash and his wife Alicia (Jennifer Connelly). Dave Bayer, professor of Mathematics at Barnard College, Columbia University, was consulted on the mathematical equations that appear in the film.

Nash's messy life is rendered simple through a seemingly straightforward narrative structure which offers a clear sense of him triumphing over adversity. The revelation of the *Sixth Sense*-twist at the end, where it is revealed that Charles (Paul Bettany) is a figment of Nash's imagination, forces the viewer to revaluate the film as a whole. The imaginary friends were an invention; yet it is unusual for schizophrenics to suffer from visual hallucinations, which are usually auditory. The change was a cinematic device to help the viewer see inside Nash's mind. His schizophrenic delusions ensure that the film's tension is retained, and viewers do not know what is real and what is imagined. As Akiva Goldsman noted, 'that John and Alicia Nash responded well to the sprit was flattering to me, but I don't pretend this is how John saw the world. This is expressing to an audience how John might have seen the world. I tried to make the delusional system more cohesive to the audience' (quoted in Divine 2002: 71).

The film was criticised for it omission of his violence, homosexuality, and making no mention of the child he had with another woman, instead offering 'a glossy example of how a troubled and troublesome life can be sanitised into a movieland saga' (Kauffman 2002). Everyone involved in the making of the film repeatedly insists that they did not intend on making a bio-pic, that it is merely inspired by Nasar's biography. The film reads more like a thriller than a life story. Goldsman continued:

> The book is straight biography and an extraordinary one. Sylvia Nasar did an amazing job. But the movie version of *A Beautiful Mind* is not a bio-pic. God gave us, in the form of John Nash, an amazing architecture of a life. Genius, madness, Nobel Prize – you can't do better than that if you're looking for drama. I tried to hang on to that architecture scenes that would evoke the experience of the life John lived, but no literal scenes from his life, there's very few of those. (Ibid.)

Yet according to Cynthia Rockwell, writing in *Cineaste* magazine,

> The book delivers a John Nash who is arrogant, selfish, unkind and unrepentant – traits that are either removed from or made charming in the film. The film does not, for example, include the fact that Nash often belittled students and colleagues as stupid if they merely asked him to clarify something: the film instead gives us a few playfully arrogant quips intended to make Nash seem endearingly socially inept rather than cruel. (2002: 36)

The narrative of the film differs wildly from Nash's actual life story with the filmmakers' emphasis on conveying Nash's mental illness, his schizophrenia and paranoia giving way to hallucinations and the imaginary friends. Nash never worked for the Pentagon; he worked between his Princeton and MIT years for the RAND corporation.

The hallucinations are shown as beginning whilst he is a student, whereas they occurred later when his wife was pregnant with their first child.

Russell Crowe as John Nash in *A Beautiful Mind* (2001)

> *A Beautiful Mind* is a thoroughly American film, a fantasy, a triumph
> of individualism over adversity. Ultimately the film is best viewed as
> its makers have contended, as a spectacle inspired by, but not loyal
> to, the film of John Nash or his biography. (Rockwell 2002: 37)

Crowe did not meet Nash prior to filming; rather he worked from seventeen
photographs. He did not want to see the seventy-year-old Nash, as he was
playing him in his late twenties over five decades earlier. The physical
changes caused by schizophrenia had a great impact on him.

The film never really explains how he won the Nobel Prize for
Mathematics. The academic content is reduced to the equations on his
classroom wall: so familiar from fictional descents-into-number-obsessive
thrillers such as *Pi* (Darren Aronofsky, 1998) and *The Number 23* (Joel
Schumacher, 2007). Russell Crowe remarked, 'Nash as he is now is not a
true witness to who he was as a younger man. We would ask questions like,
Did you ever smoke? And he would say no, and yet we know he smoked
for several years. Did you ever have a beard? Not that I can recall. And we
have photographs of him in Europe wearing a beard. From that point on, I
realised the movie would be based on broader aspects of his life' (quoted
in Palmer 2002: 46).

Nash took no medication after 1970 but the filmmakers included scenes showing that he did, as they did not want to encourage the idea that schizophrenics can overcome their illness without it. The film's moving speech at the Nobel Prize ceremony in 1994 was a Hollywood concept; he gave no such address. Further, his wife could not have been there; they had been divorced for many years, only remarrying the year the film was released. Cynthia Rockwell continues:

> The filmmakers could have avoided the criticism over authenticity had they merely changed the film's title (which is probably the film's only direct link to the book, after all). When a film is adapted from a book there are all kinds of extraordinary demands, about authenticity and loyalty, and when a film is adapted from a biography, those demands are even greater. The story is about a life actually lived, not one that is invented; therefore a certain measure of 'reality' is assumed. Biography, like documentary film, is assumed to represent fact objectively. The fact that the book's author, Sylvia Nasar, once was a reporter – with an assumed allegiance to journalistic 'fact' – adds another layer of 'authenticity' to her 'unbiased' account, and another layer of responsibility for the filmmakers. Indeed in a recent interview with *The Advocate*, Nasar admitted that she was too confused by the concept of bisexuality and had too little evidence to form any real conclusions about Nash's sexuality in her book. (Rockwell 2002: 37)

The film's budget was $58 million, it took well over $300 milion at the world-wide box office and was well received by critics.

> Director Ron Howard's approach to the problem of the biopic is totally different from Michael Mann's *Ali*. How do you make a mainstream movie out of the life of a man whose activity is almost entirely mental? Screenwriter Akiva Goldsman's clever solution is to turn the story of a troubled academic into a Hollywood thriller. How? He makes things up. Howard's movie is being touted as an Oscar contender – Hollywood loves these 'triumph of the spirit' sagas – but in 'solving' the dilemma of the biopic it's turned a fascinating life into formula. (Ansen 2001)

Kinsey (2004)

Director: Bill Condon
Screenwriter: Bill Condon
Starring: Liam Neeson (Alfred Kinsey) and Laura Linney (Clara McMillen)
Subject: American biologist, professor of entomology, zoology and sex-
    ologist Alfred Kinsey (Alfred Charles Kinsey, 1894–1956)

In 1948 Alfred Kinsey published *Sexual Behaviour in the Human Male,* an academic study on male sexual thoughts and actions. He followed this up in 1953 with a book examining the sexual behaviour of women. The book was considered so shocking that his credibility was ruined and his funding withdrawn.

    Kinsey was written and directed by the openly gay director Bill Condon, whose other bio-pics include *Gods and Monsters* (1997) about the film director James Whale and *The Fifth Estate* (2013) on Julian Assange. Condon has admitted, 'I didn't want to make the film exclusively about gayness. This would have been very much against the spirit of Kinsey's own philosophy. He believed in a great variety of forms of sexuality' (quoted in Grundmann 2005: 4).

    The film's focus is on the period leading up to the publication of Kinsey's 1948 study through to his death in 1956. The first thirty years of his life are compressed into thirteen minutes within a flashback. Here he recalls key moments from his past that helped shaped the man he had become.

    Condon based his screenplay in part on two biographies: James H. Jones's *Alfred C. Kinsey: A Public/Private Life* (1997) and Jonathan Gathorne-Hardy's *Sex the Measure of All Things: A Life of Alfred C. Kinsey* (2004). The two biographers offer contrasting conclusions about Kinsey's work. Jones claims that Kinsey's hands-on research along with an increasing personal interest in homosexuality compromised his findings whereas Gathorne-Hardy insists that Kinsey's methods were ethical and scientific. The film's position helped to redeem a man whose contribution to a greater understanding of sex, which ultimately led to the de-criminalisation of some acts, had been lost.

    Its coverage of the harsher, darker sides of Kinsey's character (his bisexuality, masochistic and voyeuristic practices) was commended by critics, but, as Roy Grundmann says, 'flawed characters make for better bio-pics' (2005: 5).

The film graphically displays Kinsey's bisexuality, his marriage to liberated and liberating Clara 'Mac' (Laura Linney) and his affair with one of his researchers Clyde Martin (Peter Sarsgaard), who later has an affair with Clara, which Kinsey endorsed. Yet, according to Grundmann, the film omits

> the fact that Kinsey recruited hundreds of 'friends of the research' (among them underground filmmaker Kenneth Anger, painters Audrey Avinoff and Paul Cadmus, and literati Glenway Wescott and Gore Vidal), who would eagerly put their address books, their porn collections, and their own bodies into the service of science. Neither does it mention the fact that Kinsey hired a gay photographer, Clarence Tripp, for the purpose of building a collection of two thousand cinematic studies of ejaculation. This is a shame, for Kinsey's reliance on gay artists and gay men in general are direct proof that his brand of science by no means preceded the wonders he discovered, but got reshaped by the concrete possibilities he encountered in the course of discovering them. (2005: 7)

The film opens with a close-up black-and-white image of Kinsey being interviewed by Clyde. As the interview continues, it becomes clear that this is a training session as Kinsey coaches his researcher on how to phrase questions, encourage responses and be aware of body language. The initial interview then triggers extended colour flashbacks to his youth, courtship of Clara, marriage and university life, which brought him to this point.

His childhood, overshadowed by recollections of his puritanical father (John Lithgow) railing against sex, science and zippers, and the young Kinsey masturbating furiously shortly after advising a fellow scout of the sinful nature of the act. Rebelling against this strict Methodist upbringing he would become the world's first expert on sexual behaviour. Another flashback shows his own awkward wedding night attempts at sex with his new bride, which leaves him ashamed and isolated. This triggers the desire to expose and understand the sex act within a variety of situations, both physiologically and psychologically.

Alongside the narrative drive of Kinsey's life are interspersed direct-to-camera addresses of his research subjects, recounting their intimate sexual desires and practices. It offers frank and graphic accounts of sexual behaviour from the standard norm to the wildly deviant.

Kinsey himself is portrayed as a flawed teacher, and poor at the politics of an academic life. Yet his talent as an interviewer ensured that his subjects revealed their most personal thoughts and feelings. The boredom of research process is exposed; and the boundaries between sexual research and the experience become blurred. The attic of his house was used, the bed had a camera trained on it, and various people perform sexual acts there as research. Yet James Christopher writes that '*Kinsey* is the most unsexy film about sex I've ever seen. ... That Condon manages to cram so much complexity and detail into this film is nothing short of astonishing' (2005).

However, the film did have its detractors. Kinsey's work, even sixty years on, is still problematic to some. Right-wing American writer Judith Riesman considered Kinsey a pervert and founder of the 'homosexual movement', dubbing him akin to Adolf Hitler and Saddam Hussein and calling for a boycott of the film. On *Kinsey*'s detractors, Condon said:

> Kinsey is such an enduring cultural figure, so I didn't want to leave out any of the stuff that makes people dislike him. I knew what the people who didn't like him were going to say, because they had been demonising him for fifty years and over the years the charges have changed. In the 1960s, it was that he was a supporter of Planned Parenthood or abortion rights or homosexual rights or that he was an atheist. In the 1980s, they landed on this totally specious charge that he was somehow a proponent of paedophilia, or in fact a paedophile himself, which of course there's no evidence for. Absolutely none. (Film4 2004b)

Condon also stated that the call for a boycott of the film 'has been a godsend for us ... I always knew that the fringe people wanted to demonise Kinsey. We've come so far since Kinsey, yet we are still in the same place. Puritanism is built into our DNA' (quoted in Goodridge 2004). An early poster for the film was banned by London Underground. It depicted Liam Neeson standing in front of phrases from Kinsey's reports including 'orgasms' and 'masturbation', the poster was withdrawn and replaced with less 'offensive' ones: 'pleasure' and 'sexually'.

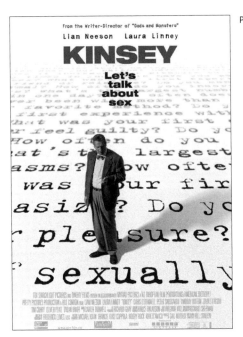

Poster for *Kinsey* (2005)

There were press reports on its world-wide certification. In Japan, it was the first film showing human genitalia to be shown uncensored, the country being known for its strict censorship policies in this area. In the US, Condon feared that the film would receive the hard-to-market NC-17, but the American ratings Board returned the film with a R rating. It was accompanied with a note saying 'Thank you, we learned a lot.'

The resulting publicity from this call for a boycott and the censorship issues surrounding the film certainly helped the box office for this relatively low-budget ($10 million) British-funded film. It was nominated widely, and won awards at specialist (GLAAD) and mainstream awards. It was also very well received critically.

Nearly every scene crams in at least two or three handy plot or character points and a quotable line or two, further proving in the wake of his previous foray into the genre – the story of horror director James Whale, *Gods and Monsters* – that Condon has a real knack for making biopics breathe. In fact, for all its daring and felicitous touches, *Kinsey* is nevertheless the kind of ruthlessly conventional movie that seems designed to woo Academy Award nominations – though surprisingly the film has missed out on Oscar recognition. (Felperin 2005).

Further viewing

Creation (John Amiel, 2009); Charles Darwin (Paul Bettany)
A Dangerous Method (David Cronenberg, 2011); Sigmund Freud (Viggo
    Mortensen) and Carl Jung (Michael Fassbender)
October Sky (Joe Johnston, 1999); Homer Hickam (Jake Gyllenhaal)

7 INTO THE STORM: THE POLITICS OF
POLITICAL BIO-PICS

A political biopic should seek to provide intimate insight into a
real human being. Their surge in popularity is arguably a reflec-
tion of society's desire to see our political figures in real terms
and thus avoid the tendency to label them as simply good or bad;
wrong or right.

> – Rebecca Lloyd, *The New Statesman* (2011)

The films analysed in this chapter focus on three contrasting politicians:
Richard Nixon, Abraham Lincoln and Nelson Mandela.

Certainly no one would argue that Richard Nixon is an important figure
in American politics. Oliver Stone's bio-pic, *Nixon* (1995), is a big sweeping
epic, its fragmented narrative and visual style dominated by the performance of Anthony Hopkins as the tragic president. It was criticised for its
length and for the final hour, focusing on the minutiae of the Watergate
scandal. Here we will focus on Morgan and Howard's *Frost/Nixon* (2008)
which manages to combine both the importance of Nixon pre- and post-
Watergate in a highly entertaining peek behind-the-scenes of the machinations of the infamous 1977 interview where Frost manages to an elicit an
apology (of sorts) from Nixon.

Abraham Lincoln has been the subject of countless films, from presi-
dential bio-pics such as *Young Mr. Lincoln* (John Ford, 1939) to the action-

adventurer in *Abraham Lincoln, Vampire Hunter* (Timur Bekmambetov, 2010) where he combines his full-time job as President, with the part-time one of vampire hunter. In 2012 Daniel Day-Lewis played him in a film version directed by Steven Speilberg.

Nelson Mandela has been hailed as the 'Lincoln of Africa'. He was portrayed by Danny Glover in *Mandela* (1987) and since his election victory in 1994, by Sidney Poitier in *Mandela and de Klerk* (1997), Dennis Haysbert in *Goodbye Bafana* (2007), David Harewood in *Mrs Mandela* (2010), Morgan Freeman in *Invictus* (2009), Terrence Howard in *Winnie Mandela* (2011) and Idris Elba in *Mandela: Long Walk to Freedom* (2013). Here we will look at two of these, one which focuses on one year (*Invictus*) and the other that covers almost sixty years (*Mandela: Long Walk to Freedom*).

Frost/Nixon (2008)

Director: Ron Howard
Screenwriter: Peter Morgan
Starring: Michael Sheen (David Frost) and Frank Langella (Richard Nixon)
Subject: American president Richard Nixon (Richard Milhous Nixon,
    1913–1994) and English journalist David Frost (Sir David Paradine
    Frost, 1939–2013)

In 2008 Michael Sheen and Frank Langella reproduced their 2006 West End and Broadway stage performances on film for director Ron Howard, from Peter Morgan's screenplay based on his play. It portrays Frost as a jet-setting lightweight TV personality whose career was in decline. This was 'far from the truth' says Frost who had interviewed prime ministers, presidents and religious leaders, and by 1977 had done over 4,000 interviews, including one in 1968 with Nixon (see Hoyle 2008).

With his political career over, low on funds and his memoirs about to be published, the film posits that Nixon's publicist, Swifty Lazar (Toby Jones) felt that a series of television interviews would aid the book's promotion, and sought payment for a series of interviews. The highest bid of $600,000 and a 20% share of the profits came from David Frost's production company.

One of the film's most problematic scenes from those seeking historical accuracy was the late-night telephone call a seemingly drunk Nixon makes to Frost in which he talks about 'being looked down on'. This was a complete fabrication by Morgan. Jonathan Aitken, Nixon's biographer says,

> Those of us who were around at the time are united in our incredulity over three major historical flaws in the Hollywood version of the story. Without giving too much of the plot away, the most dramatic twist in the movie comes when Nixon makes an extraordinary and emotional late-night phone call to Frost. This phone call did not happen. Nixon's weird rant about his personal motivations and social resentments, which purportedly gave Frost new clues to hidden secrets about the Watergate cover-up, is, from start to finish, an artistic invention by the scriptwriter Peter Morgan. He uses this dramatic device as the turning-point which gave a demoralised Frost fresh hope and adrenaline, firing up his psyche so that he became transformed into a pugnacious interrogator whose brutal line of questioning ultimately broke the former President. (2009)

Morgan explains its inclusion:

> Do I think the phone call between David Frost and Richard Nixon is truthful? Absolutely. Is it accurate? Absolutely not. Did it happen? No. Could it have happened? Yes. In that scene we find out why David Frost is as ambitions as he is and why Richard Nixon is as ambitious as he is. It asks what the difference between these two men are, what deceives them, what haunts them, what makes them human. (Quoted in Teeman 2009)

Author of *Nixonland: The Rise of a President and the Fracturing of America*, Rick Perlstein said:

> The film conveys the poetic truth of who Nixon was magnificently. They got his shambling physical awkwardness, which he learned to overcome when the camera was on. The scene where he has the phone conversation with Frost in the hotel late at night quite splendidly captures his political identity, and his ability to reach out to people by speaking to the common condition of being condescended to. (2009)

Frank Langella as Richard Nixon in *Frost/Nixon* (2008)

Although he agreed to do the interviews, and was being paid, Nixon managed to stonewall many of Frost's questions or give long meaningless answers. There was 29 hours of filmed material, which were transmitted in summer 1977 as four ninety-minute programmes watched by 45 million people. The real answer to Frost's three questions at the end is closer to twenty minutes in reality, and does not end with the signature 'shattered man' close-up as portrayed by Frank Langella. Howard applied a similar shooting and editing sensibility to the interviews as he had done to the boxing sequences in *Cinderella Man* (2005).

Critics have complained that Peter Morgan has oversimplified the story. But in researching the play, he interviewed everyone involved and they all had different story to tell. He does, naturally edit the interview for dramatic effect: 'There's 10 or 12% of fiction in these, one or two bits of which I could do without' Frost remarked; he described it as 'brilliant', however he regrets that 'to build up the underdog thing' Peter Morgan downplayed his distinguished TV career (quoted in Hoyle 2008).

Other script changes for dramatic purposes were a re-ordering of the interview topics, those covering Watergate were days 8 and 9 (of 12). Unlike the film, where researchers' discover at the last minute Nixon's conversations with Charles Colson, Special Counsel to President Nixon from 1969 to 1973, known as his 'Hatchet Man', this fact had been known for eight months and were not considered to be as significant as the film implies.

The film was released in December 2008 to good reviews. It took $27 million world-wide; its budget was $25 million.

The film's authorial voice is once again Peter Morgan's:

> It's hard to argue that Howard brings anything new to Morgan's play. Perhaps his biggest achievement is to preserve the fine performances of Michael Sheen and Frank Langella, who both starred in the original London theatre production. What the director of *Apollo 13* and *Cinderella Man* does find in Morgan's typically bold and witty script is an energetic sports movie, with an underdog, Frost, who flounders for three quarters before triumphing in the fourth, along the way indulging in sweaty close-ups, ample pep talks and an extended training period. (Calhoun 2009)

Michael Sheen, unsurprisingly, received much acclaim, and captured the swooping vocals of Frost so familiar to UK audiences:

> Michael Sheen, Britain's smartest chameleon, has a feel for the torn edges of loudmouths — his Kenneth Williams was caustic and brittle, his Tony Blair quick witted and edgy, and we can but greedily anticipate his forthcoming stint as egocentric football whiz Brian Clough for *The Damned United*. As Frost, Sheen gives first the camp exterior then the moral voice mustering its strength like Hulk ready to rip through his silk shirts. It's a magnificent announcement of a performance — a pitch-perfect impression and a layered character, a hero spotted with vanity. His battle with Nixon made Frost a world player; its fictional counterpart could make Sheen our finest export. (Nathan 2009: 62)

In the US, it was Frank Langella that was fêted. The film was nominated for five Academy Awards, including Frank Langella for Best Actor, but failed to win in any category.

Lincoln (2012)

Director: Steven Spielberg
Screenwriter: Tony Kushner
Starring: Daniel Day-Lewis (Abraham Lincoln) and Sally Field (Mary Todd Lincoln)

Daniel Day-Lewis as Abraham Lincoln in *Lincoln* (2012)

Subject: American President, Abraham Lincoln (1809–1865)

Lincoln is based in part on Doris Kearns Goodwin's biography *Team of Rivals: The Political Genius of Abraham Lincoln* (2005), which Spielberg had optioned in 2001.

In 2005, John Logan was hired to write a script based around Lincoln's friendship with African-American social reformer Frederick Douglass. In January 2006, playwright Paul Webb was brought in to re-work this script, widening the narrative scope to cover a wider period of Lincoln's life, and Liam Neeson was cast as Lincoln. Over the next five years Spielberg continued to work on the film, now with Tony Kusher, to find a cinematic way into Lincoln's work and life. Kusher's 2009 script focused on the final four months of Lincoln's life in early 1865, when he was trying to have the Thirteenth Amendment to the United States Constitution passed by the United States House of Representatives. The Thirteenth Amendment would see slavery and involuntary servitude abolished except as punishment for a crime. It was this approach that would be filmed. Neeson, by this point, felt he was too old to play Lincoln, and in November 2010, Day-Lewis was cast.

The film covers the period from January to April 1865. It opens on the battlefields of the Civil War amidst its bloody hand-to-hand combat; this segues to two black soldiers recounting their experiences to an unknown superior. The camera pulls back to reveal that they are addressing Lincoln, visiting the front line in January 1896. This Lincoln is world-weary, but clearly still dedicated to seeing a swift end to the war. He believes that the Civil

War is drawing to a conclusion, and that his Emancipation Proclamation drawn up in 1863 may be disregarded in some states, and that freed slaves will be returned to slavery. The narrative of *Lincoln* follows the next four months as he negotiates with both parties to get the Thirteen Amendment passed. This would be his final act, as he was assassinated at the Ford Theatre in April 1865.

By using this momentous period of world history as the basis, the film-makers extrapolate wider issues of Lincoln's political machinations and character – and those who surround him. Day-Lewis portrays Lincoln with dignity and gravitas, but with an underlying thread of humour which makes him human: he has his speech under his hat, gives him youngest son Tad (Gulliver McGrath) piggy-back-rides and forgets his slippers. Spielberg said:

> I didn't want to make a movie about a statue. I wanted him to be flesh and bone – to see the President's thought processes. You get to exist with him, for long moments where nothing is said. He spent a lot of time in the deeps. Sometimes the deeps were cold. Other times, there were in retreat. (Quoted in Shone 2013)

The film ends with a flashback, with Lincoln delivering his second inaugural address (March 1865). With victory and the end of the Civil War in sight, he speaks of the sadness which saw the country ripped apart. He calls for peace, declares that this war would have no victors and speaks of the unmistakable evil of slavery, little realising that in the crowd are the men who would plot and carry out his assassination a month later.

The film opened in November 2012 to universal critical acclaim. Its budget of $65 million was quickly recouped as it took over $275 million world-wide. Both the film and its actors were nominated for major awards, with Day-Lewis collecting 21 acting awards.

> In a towering performance, Day-Lewis encompasses the great statesman who shaped history, the intimate man of the people and the mysterious, charismatic figure. (French 2013)

Harold Holzer, co-chair of the Abraham Lincoln Bicentennial Foundation was a consultant on the film; he acknowledged that there some small historical inaccuracies: Mary Lincoln would never have visited the House of Representatives, Lincoln would never have retrieved his speech from the lining of his top hat, nor would anyone have been able to recite the words of the Gettysburg Address. But ends by saying, 'There is no doubt that Spielberg has travelled toward an understanding of Abraham Lincoln more boldly than any other filmmaker before him' (2012).

Allen Guelzo, a professor of the Civil War era, stated that

the film was 90 percent on the mark, which given the way Hollywood usually does history is saying something. I thought that it got with reasonable accuracy a lot of Lincoln's character, the characters of the main protagonists, and the overall debate over the Thirteenth Amendment. The acting and screenwriting were especially well done. I remember thinking afterwards that all the time I'd been watching the movie I had never thought that Daniel Day-Lewis was acting, because what he portrayed seemed so close to my own mental image of what Lincoln must have been like. (Quoted in Mackaman 2013)

Invictus (2009)

Director: Clint Eastwood
Screenwriter: Anthony Peckham
Starring: Morgan Freeman (Nelson Mandela) and Matt Damon (Francois Pienaar)

[and]

Mandela: Long Walk to Freedom (2013)

Director: Justin Chadwick
Screenwriter: William Nicholson
Starring: Idris Elba (Nelson Mandela) and Naomie Harris (Winnie Mandela)
Subject: South African President Nelson Mandela (Nelson Rolihlahla Mandela 1918–2014)

Invictus is based on John Carlin's non-fiction book *Playing the Enemy: Mandela and the Game that Made a Nation* (2008). He met Freeman (who bought the rights to the book) through a friend and pitched him the idea. Carlin started with, 'I have a movie for you. It's based on a book I am writing about an event that distils the essence of the South African miracle.' Before Carlin could go further Freeman responded 'Oh, you mean the rugby game?' (2010). He had wanted to play Mandela for several years, as he knew and admired him, and was aware of Carlin's work-in-progress. Freeman had bought the rights to Mandela's autobiography, *Long Walk to Freedom*, but no screenwriter had managed to shape a screenplay from the vast material. In the summer of 2007, Freeman, with Carlin's book in hand, went to Clint Eastwood with the idea for the film. Eastwood called Matt Damon who signed up right away. Eighteen months later, filming began in South Africa in March 2009 and it ended on May.

Eastwood said, 'I love the fact that the story is concise, that you don't have to go back and see him as a young man, the thing with Winnie, and all that stuff' (ibid.). Indeed, rather than a straight bio-pic, it is a powerful film about the power of sports and national pride. It also follows the familiar sport-film narrative of the underdog made good. At the film's outset the Springboks are portrayed as a failing team with little hope of succeeding in the 1995 Rugby World Cup they are about to host. Francois Pienaar is captain of an unfit team, boycotted internationally for years, frequently facing humiliation.

Ed Griffiths, Chief Executive of the South African Rugby Union and communication director of the South African team during the 1995 World Cup stated:

Invictus does accurately reflect the spirit of that tournament, and I know because I was there every day. ... It was a month that seemed surreal – because a country that had been so divided did come together. It might sound sugary to suggest that, but for that month it absolutely did. But the idea that the World Cup was part of some preconceived grand plan for the Rainbow Nation – which is the central theme of the movie – is just not accurate. There was no grand plan. It just happened. Call it destiny. It was a spontaneous result of a number of special people, most prominent of whom were Mandela and Pienaar, coming together in an event that prompted extraordinary emotions around South Africa and indeed around the rugby world. There is no question that Mandela saw in the World Cup an opportunity to bring the country together and he held the country to it brilliantly. (2010)

What he disputes is that Mandela and Pienaar met and planned this.

The film follows a familiar trajectory. It opens with a prologue of Mandela's release from prison in 1990. As he is driven from the prison, he passes by a long fence; on one side of the road, young black children are playing football on a lumpy wasteland, on the other privileged white South Africans are playing rugby on manicured grounds. The rugby coach turns to one of this young players and says, 'this is the day our country went to the dogs', highlighting the engrained hatred and fear some white South Africans held for black South Africans. With precision and clarity, Eastwood effectively laid the touch-stone for the film's main themes: social division and fear. This opening scene exemplifies the nation's apartheid, and established sporting preferences: white South Africans' love of rugby and black South Africans' for football. Indeed, when it came to rugby, the black South Africans would support any team other than the Springboks.

Through a montage of archive footage we see a South Africa divided, fuelled by violence and hatred, which segues to Mandela giving a speech calling for unification. In 1994, the polls open for all South Africans, and Mandela is voted in as President.

Once inaugurated he sets about dismantling the legacy of apartheid. Tackling institutionalised racism (from both black and white South Africans) he gives a moving speech on his first day in office. He sees an opportunity to unify further when at a rugby match he sees and recalls

Morgan Freeman as Nelson Mandela in *Invictus* (2009)

that black South Africans are cheering not for the Springboks, but for the other team. He meets with Francois Pienaar, the captain of the South Africa rugby union team, and inspires him to work towards winning the World Cup that they will be hosting. There follows a series of training sequences and PR exercises as the 'hated' Springboks go out into the townships to coach the children. Meanwhile, Mandela makes public his support for them.

The narrative structure and message is simple. We forget that we are watching history; sport is the catalyst/backdrop to a much larger drama. Yet the political and social importance of this moment in history reflects the wider issues of the black majority's yearning for revenge and the fear the white minority has of retaliation. Mandela's desire for reconciliation is resolute and his actions here resonate. Mandela understood that the way to beat one's enemy is not to destroy them but to win them over.

The film does not use any flashbacks to show Mandela's or South Africa's recent past. Nor does it touch on Mandela's marital concerns which were being made public at this time. The only visual reference to Mandela's incarceration is a sequence when the Springboks go to the Robben Island prison. Pienaar, affected by the visit, imagines Mandela there. In a fantasy sequence he sees a ghost-like image of Mandela in the cell, out in the yard smashing rocks, while a voiceover narrates the nineteenth-century poem 'Invictus' (Latin for 'invincible'), that Mandela had given to Pienaar as inspiration. In reality Pienaar was given a copy of the 'The Man in the Arena' passage from President of the United States Theodore Roosevelt's speech, 'Citizenship in a Republic'.

John Carlin, on whose book, the film was based, said, 'The first time I saw the film, having been terrified that they'd fuck it up, I just sat there as the credits rolled with a lump in my throat. I've never felt so proud in my life' (quoted in Cohen 2010). Yet Carlin had received some criticism. Left-wing journalist John Pilger felt that he essentially written a hagiography to which Carlin responded: 'It's difficult not to do a hagiography. Mandela is to politics what Mozart is to music. He is the Abraham Lincoln of our times. And the great good fortune of my working life has been to know him. I'm telling his story, all that I can do is to be honest' (ibid.).

Freeman delivers an understated performance which catches the dignity, wit, wisdom and cheekiness one associates with the elder states-man, a performance for which he was nominated for many acting awards. *Invictus* was not as big a hit in the US as it was overseas. Its budget was

$60 million, and it took $37.5 million in the US, and almost $85 million internationally.

> Politically significant true-life story? Check. Triumph over adversity? Check. Wrongs righted? Craggy old man in role of a lifetime? Directed by US national treasure? Sport as metaphor? Checkity, check check. What could be more high-fivingly all-American? Well, perhaps, that it's centred on the 1995 Rugby World Cup – a sport even more unpopular in the US than 'soccer'. (DG 2010: 41)

Three years later, director Justin Chadwick, producers Anant Singh and David Thompson, with screenwriter William Nicholson finally brought the long anticipated 'official' version of Mandela's autobiography, *Mandela: Long Walk to Freedom*, to the screen. It serves as a prequel, of sorts, to *Invictus*, as it ends at the point of his election, and traces his journey from childhood, his years as an apolitical/womanising lawyer, his abandonment of his first wife and child, his relationship with his second wife Winnie, his growing involvement in the ANC, his arrest and trial, his 27-year incarceration on Robben Island and negotiations for release.

Eschewing approaches from major American studios, Mandela finally placed his trust in a British/South African co-production. *Mandela: Long Walk to Freedom* had its world premiere at the Toronto Film Festival in September 2013; it opened in South Africa and on a limited released in the US on 28 November. It had its UK premiere on 5 December 2013 at a Royal Gala Performance in the presence of the Duke and Duchess of Cambridge and Mandela's daughters Zindzi and Zenani. Whilst the film was being shown, news reached them of Mandela's death. During the closing credits, producer Anant Singh and actor Idris Elba took to the stage and informed the audience that Mandela had died. Prince William made a brief statement to the press as he left the screening: 'I just wanted to say it's extremely sad and tragic news. We were just reminded what an extraordinary and inspiring man Nelson Mandela was. My thoughts and prayers are with him and his family right now.'

In the intervening month before its UK release, there had been much speculation and anticipation regarding the film's critical, box office and awards success. This official/endorsed film surely must be a fitting final tribute to a man who made such an impact on his own country, and as an inter-

Idris Elba as Nelson Mandela in *Mandela: Long Walk to Freedom* (2013)

national statesman and diplomat. The film opened in the UK on 3 January 2014. There was praise for Elba's performance, but the reviews were 'average'. The film's structure and narrative drive to tell the whole story offers a by-the-numbers, 'greatest-hits' narrative. The filmmakers obvious reverence for the subject matter pours forth, yet it does not shy away from the darker, earlier years. The compression of the 27 years of incarceration, and the underdevelopment of characters that surround him, left audiences underwhelmed. Yet this is Mandela's story, using his autobiography as its primary source, so any criticism of historical inaccuracy or bias, should be levelled at the autobiography and the reluctance of the film to offer contradictory views.

The film opens with an older Mandela reciting a dream and saying 'they never see me'. The narration continues as we return to a prologue of his childhood (he is played here by Sizi Pini) in the honey-hued Xhosa region, and a tribal ritual of young men (now played by Atandwa Kani) saying goodbye to their childhood and he is given the name 'troublemaker'. He says, 'I didn't want to make too much trouble, [just] make my family proud.' The story then moves to 1942, Johannesburg, where Mandela (now played by Idris Elba) is a young lawyer making a name for himself. The death of a friend in police custody sparks a desire to agitate for reform. Incensed by the increased military presence and segregation in the townships, he starts giving speeches in support of the African National Congres (ANC). He also becomes violent towards his wife, who subsequently leaves him. He then meets and gets engaged to Winnie. In 1960 at a demonstration in Sharpeville where black South Africans were burning passports in defiance of new regulations, soldiers start shooting at the crowd and hundreds are injured and killed. It is this event that forces him to become more radical and go underground, as the movement becomes increasingly violent. He and his associates are captured and put on trial in Pretoria in 1963. Not wishing them to become martyrs they are given life imprisonment and are sent to Robben Island in July 1964.

At this point we see scenes that would have been beyond Mandela's point of view. Winnie visits and tells him of her arrests, which we are shown, and see her increasingly politicised by the violence and persecution mounted upon her. The film does show some of the violence meted upon Winnie whilst being interrogated and her growing extreme political activism (at odds with that of Mandela) but it does not dwell on this, or her affairs. This was covered effectively in the BBC film *Mrs Mandela* with Sophie Okonedo (Michael Samuels, 2010), which shows Winnie Mandela's transformation from a shy country girl in her twenties to a head-strong woman in her fifties. This thoughtful drama does not excuse her for her later criminal activities, but does offer an explanation for it. Darrell Roodt with Jennifer Hudson in *Winnie* (2011) does shy away from fully exploring Winnie as war criminal, but offers very graphic depictions of the violence of the riots meted on the black South Africans which triggers her extremism.

We see more of life outside of Mandela's purview as archive footage of the anti-apartheid movement becomes greater, world leaders speaking out against South Africa's segregation; there are trade restrictions, a 'Free Nelson Mandela' campaign is launched, and a concert planned to coincide with his seventieth birthday. These lead to secret negotiations on Mandela's release and on 11 February 1990 he is set free, with Winnie at his side. It soon becomes apparent that their politics have diverged and he says, 'I love her as she was, not how she has become.' The film ends with his election in April 1994. The framing device of the dream returns and the voice-over ends by saying, 'learn to love, taught to love'.

The budget was $35 million with the film taking $27 million box office on its theatrical release. The reviews were concerned about the apparent reverence of the piece.

Unless a filmmaker opts for the impressionistic approach, the best this genre can hope for is a *Reader's Digest* abridgement, a pulped and potted novelisation. Luckily it has Elba, who can convey in one loaded look several pages' worth of pathos, inner conflict, stoicism or resolve. (Gilbey 2014)

Let the words 'Cry freedom' ring across the world. Freedom from political cruelty and oppression. But freedom too, please, from hagiographical stinkers like *Mandela: Long Walk to Freedom*. Stinkers that smell no better because they have an earnest, honourable, bleeding-heart subject. Poor Nelson Mandela. Barely in the ground and one more giant clod of well-meant, pious banality is thrown on his memory. Couldn't we have had some controversy-stirring candour about this true-life hero in his early terrorist phase? British actor Idris Elba expends his skills on painstaking vocal mimicry, leaving none for emotion, spontaneity or a simulation of intellectual vitality. (Andrews 2014)

Further viewing

Amazing Grace (Michael Apted, 2006); William Wilberforce (Ioan Gruffudd)
The Butler (Lee Daniels, 2013); Cecil Gaines (Forest Whitaker)
César Chávez (Diego Luna, 2014); César Chávez (Michael Peña)
Che, parts 1 and 2 (Steven Soderbergh, 2008); Ernesto 'Che' Guevara (Benicio Del Toro)
Downfall (Olivier Hirschbiegel, 2004); Adolf Hitler (Bruno Ganz)
Evita (Alan Parker, 1996); Eva Peron (Madonna)
The Iron Lady (Phyllida Lloyd, 2012); Margaret Thatcher (Meryl Streep)
J. Edgar (Clint Eastwood, 2011); J. Edgar Hoover (Leonardo DiCaprio)
The Last King of Scotland (Kevin MacDonald, 2006); Idi Amin (Forest Whittaker)
Milk (Gus Van Sant, 2009); Harvey Milk (Sean Penn)
The Motorcycle Diaries (Walter Salles, 2004); Ernesto 'Che' Guevara (Gael Garcia Bernal)
Mrs Mandela (Michael Samuels, 2010); Winnie Mandela (Sophie Okonedo) and Nelson Mandela (David Harewood)
Nixon (Oliver Stone, 1995); Richard Nixon (Anthony Hopkins)
W (Oliver Stone, 2008); George Bush (Josh Brolin)
Winnie (Darrell Roodt, 2011); Winnie Mandela (Jennifer Hudson) and Nelson (Terrence Howard)

8   A ROYAL AFFAIR: THE MAJESTY OF ROYAL
       REPRESENTATIONS

Often the female royal figure must choose between her heart and
her 'professional' commitment to the state. The mere owning up to
sexual desire is often taken, by men, as a sign of weakness, so a
female ruler can only show her mettle by forgoing things typically
'female'.

— George F. Custen, *Bio/Pics:*
How Hollywood Constructed Public History (1992: 105)

Royal bio-pics have been a mainstay of commercial cinema since its
inception. Historians fear them as, ultimately, they are seen as a commercial and entertainment venture first and historical document second.
Inevitably filmmakers will have to condense, elide, edit and re-organise a
life in order to make a satisfactory and coherent narrative. They are usually
held up as exemplars of high production values in costume, hair, make-up,
set design and location. Stately homes which are used as locations often
subsequently see a high up-turn in visitor numbers.

Here, we will be examining four films examining the lives of queens
which exemplify Custen's thesis of pitting their private and public personas
against one another: an Asian director's take on English history with his
pair of films on Elizabeth I starring the Australian actress, Cate Blanchett;
American director Sofia Coppola's version of French history in *Marie*

Antoinette with Kirsten Dunst; and the British director Stephen Frears' examination of a short period in the life of Elizabeth II in *The Queen*.

Elizabeth (1998) and Elizabeth: The Golden Age (2007)

Director: Shekhar Kapur
Screenwriters: Michael Hirst (*Elizabeth* and *Elizabeth: The Golden Age*) and William Nicholson (*Elizabeth: The Golden Age*)
Starring: Cate Blanchett (Elizabeth) and Geoffrey Rush (Sir Francis Walsingham)
Subject: Queen Elizabeth of England and Ireland (1533–1603)

Films about Elizabeth I have been a popular cinematic subject. The first was Sarah Bernhardt's *Queen Elizabeth* (1912), in which she improbably dies of a broken heart after learning of the Earl of Essex's death. Bette Davis played Elizabeth twice: in *The Private Lives of Elizabeth and Essex* (1939) with Errol Flynn as Essex, and in *The Virgin Queen* (1955) which focuses on her romancing of Sir Walter Raleigh (Richard Todd). Flora Robson played Elizabeth in two films: *Fire Over England* (1936) and *The Sea Hawk* (1940) – both focusing on the 1588 attack of the Spanish Armada. Jean Simmons played a teenage Elizabeth in *Young Bess* (1953), which saw the fourteen-year-old princess being seduced by the much older Thomas Seymour (Stewart Granger).

According to the on-screen titles, *Elizabeth* (1998) covers the period of her reign from 1554 to 1563 (the closing credits stating that she reigned for a further forty years). However, a number of the historical incidents that appear in the film are outside of this time frame, including the Duke of Norfolk's execution (1572) and the Duke of Anjou's appearance in Court (1571). Geoffrey Rush, who plays Sir Francis Walsingham, stated: '[Kapur] wants to tell the story of a young woman torn between love and duty, testing her emotional and political dominions. And if some fifteen-year-old student comes out of the film and disputes the facts, then I think that's great. Shekhar's interested in chaos – he's added chaos to history' (quoted in Charity 1998).

Although some of these events have been brought forward, the intention of the filmmaker is clear: to create a direct path from young carefree princess to Gloriana, the Virgin Queen. Shekhar Kapur has said:

Cate Blanchett as Elizabeth I in *Elizabeth* (1998)

All history is interpretation. It intrigues me how people are still hung up on the fact that Elizabeth was a virgin even now. Why is that so important to people? Here is a woman who had four fairly well-documented relationships, and everybody insists she was a virgin. It must be a political thing. The denial of sexuality somehow makes a woman greater. (Ibid.)

It was unlikely that Elizabeth ever had an affair with Dudley (as shown here), nor was she likely to have been a 'virgin'.

This was Kapur's first film in English; his previous film, *The Bandit Queen* (1994) having earned him an international reputation. Rush noted that, 'Shekhar had no cultural reverence for English history. Coming from Bombay, he has a good perspective on how extreme London might have been 450 years ago' (ibid.).

As the title implies, the film is seen from Elizabeth's point of view and we witness her change in attitude and appearance. The first shots of the film are of a dream-like sunlit-dappled group of young women with flowing dresses and an abundance of golden curls. They are frolicking in a meadow, free from all affairs of state and political machinations that the young princess will soon find herself embroiled in. As Queen she increasingly takes on more responsibility and this maturity is made manifest visually in the change of style of her dresses, make-up and hairstyles which become ever-more corseted and restrictive. In the final scene her hair is being shorn. She has sacrificed love and marriage, pronouncing, 'See, I have become a virgin. I am married to England.'

Once in the court, there is a sense of unease and dread, danger lurking in every dark shadow as various plots are planned and executed. The theme of conflict resonates; conflicts between Catholics and Protestants, Mary and Elizabeth, love and duty. Her advisor William Cecil (Richard Attenborough) attempts to make advantageous marriage pairings, including the Duke of Anjou (Vincent Cassell) and Catholic Philip II of Spain (George Yiasoumi), but it is the young and highly inappropriate Robert Dudley (Joseph Fiennes) with whom she is shown having an affair.

Jane Dunn author of *Elizabeth and Mary, Cousins, Rivals, Queens* (2003) said:

> I love what Cate did [here] ... I think she was extremely moving in the lead role. Having said that, the history in the first film was bunkum. It was mixed up and unnecessarily wrong. I fear that they will try and sex things up. The remarkable thing about Elizabeth was not that she jumped into bed with every man she met but that she so effectively resisted temptation. People did speculate that she slept with Raleigh, among others, but they also speculated that she was incapable of physically making love to anyone. There is no evidence that she slept with any man. (Quoted in Hastings 2005)

The film was released a few months after the Elizabethan romp *Shakespeare in Love* and shares two cast members: Geoffrey Rush and Joseph Fiennes. It did well at the box office, and proved to be an international platform for the then relatively unknown Cate Blanchett, who won eleven major awards, including a BAFTA. The coveted Best Actress Academy Award was given to Gwyneth Paltrow for her role of Viola De Lesseps in the Elizabethan-set romp *Shakespeare in Love*, which Wendy Ide described as 'One of the greatest travesties in the recent history of awards' (2007). In the same ceremony Judi Dench won a Best Supporting Actress Academy Award for her twelve minutes of screen-time as Elizabeth I in *Shakespeare in Love*.

The film's agenda is not primarily historical accuracy but rather to depict a complex period of political history in an engaging manner. It was marketed in the UK as a political thriller and the film utilises elements of the genre within the narrative and cinematography. The Duke of Norfolk (Christopher Eccleston) is shown to be a sexual and political predator and places himself at the centre of the drama, whereas Sir Francis Walsingham is forever in the shadows pursuing his enigmatic agenda.

It has a contemporary editing style (by Gill Bilcock) who edited Baz Luhrmann's *Romeo + Juliet* (1996) which Kapur much admired. The sound design mirrors this as traditional instruments are used alongside synthe-sisers and sound effects of unsettling howls of wind and off-screen cries in echo chambers further bring out the thriller elements. These marked it out as different from the slew of heritage films that had been released, most notably those under the banner of Merchant Ivory.

This thriller tone was continued in the film's UK poster campaign which featured large tinted black and white images of the four leads with a one word summary of their place within the drama: Elizabeth – heretic; Norfolk – traitor; Walsingham – assassin; Dudley – lover; all very similar in style to the *Trainspotting* poster campaign in 1995. The poster's tagline read 'Declared illegitimate Aged 3. Tried for treason Aged 21. Crowned Queen Aged 25.'

In the US the poster used a full colour image of the young Elizabeth, casually draped in a chair, connoting a sexually confident young woman. There, Alison Owen, the film's producer, pitched it as '*Trainspotting* meets *The Godfather* meets British royalty'. It was well-received, particularly with American women who 'responded far more excitedly to the character of Elizabeth, whereas here [in the UK] people came away from the first screenings feeling they couldn't identify with her. In America, women were jumping out of their seats shouting "Go girl!"' (quoted in Marriott 1998).

The film would gross $82 million world-wide, a good return on its $15 million budget. Owen said: 'The movies that do well in the States tend to present the popular picture of England. Americans have got preconcep-tions about England being all Beefeaters and Nelson's Column. Elizabeth has that element of history, so they feel at home' (ibid.).

It was critically well-received on both sides of the Atlantic.

Brimming with royal intrigue, court conspiracies, sex, violence, treachery, bloodshed and even a touch of cross-dressing, *Elizabeth* is superior historical soap opera that shrewdly sidesteps all the clichés of British costume drama with its bold, often modern approach. Propelled by Shekhar Kapur's muscular direction, by Michael Hirst's witty script and, perhaps most significant, by Cate Blanchett's remarkable performance as the Virgin Queen who ruled England for more than forty years, this richly entertaining saga is accessible enough to go beyond upscale crowds and possibly find wider appeal. (Rooney 1998)

Elizabeth is no dead slab of cinema. The film offers a new brand of history, styled to catch the attention of restless modern youth ... this may suggest a variety show, full of stunt effects and cute casting. But *Elizabeth* is an organic and intelligent whole, suavely shot and performed, made with as much concern for modern sensibilities as for its selected facts of history. (Brown 1998)

Almost ten years later, Cate Blanchett reprised her BAFTA-winning, Academy Award-nominated role of Elizabeth, now a mature, statelier Queen.

The film starts almost ten years after the last one ended and follows her open challenge by Philip II of Spain (Jordi Molia), the figurehead of European Catholicism. The political intrigues of the Court continue. Her femininity would have had an impact on her perceived effectiveness as a ruler, she is portrayed as a career-woman with no interest in producing an heir which concerns her advisors. Elizabeth positioned herself as the gender-neutral Monarch, rather than Queen, usually considered the wife to a King. Assassination plots are uncovered, orchestrated we are led to believe by Mary Queen of Scots (Samantha Morton), which ultimately leads to her death. The film ends with the English defeat of the Spanish Armada. Neither Sir Francis Drake nor the Duke of Medina Sidnoia are featured in this grand finale, despite both being there in reality. However, Walter Raleigh (Clive Owen) does perform spectacular heroics worthy of any Douglas Fairbanks Jr or Errol Flynn movie – despite there being no documentary evidence that he was even there.

More inaccuracies include the depiction of Mary Queen of Scots being executed soon after her arrest, whereas in reality she was imprisoned for nineteen years; Dr Dee did not advise Elizabeth until after the defeat of the Armada; and no English ships were lost during the battle. Characters' ages vary greatly from what they would have been at this period and as with the first film, some historically recorded events that happened earlier or later than the time period are incorporated into the film's narrative timeline.

Although Blanchett's performance was once again praised, critics and historians found the bias and presentation of historical fact troubling. Its overly melodramatic feel was also questioned, many deriding the scene in which Elizabeth dressed in gleaming armour and with her red hair flowing, arrives astride a horse at the cliff-tops to give her troops a rallying speech; this is a purely cinematic conceit. Screenwriter William Nicholson says, 'My screenplay centres on a woman whose hopes of love are in conflict with her hold on power' (2007).

Some UK critics gave a rating as low as 'one star' saying, 'Where Kapur's first Elizabeth was cool, cerebral, fascinatingly concerned with complex plotting, the new movie is pitched at the level of a Jean Plaidy romantic novel' (Bradshaw 2007b). Others questioned its tone, but nevertheless urged audiences to see it for Blanchett's performance which offers 'soulful modulation between queenly command and womanly anguish' (Quinn 2007).

Professor Cardini (a Vatican-endorsed historian) condemned the film as a 'distorted anti-papal travesty. A film which so profoundly and perversely falsifies history that it cannot be judged a good film' (quoted in Owen 2007). He had particular concern over the presentation of King Philip II of Spain who was shown as a 'ferocious, fanatical Catholic, swinging his rosary like a weapon and roaming the Escorial Palace like a madman, full of impotent fury, dreaming of subjugating the world of catholic faith'; in contrast Elizabeth was portrayed as an 'able politician and courageous sovereign', failing to show that she 'exterminated the Catholics of Scotland and Ireland' (ibid.).

The estimated budget of around $55 million reflects the focus on spectacle. The sumptuous visuals call to mind the look of oil paintings of the Tudor, Elizabethan and Jacobean period. It made $74 million at the box office, not entirely replicating its predecessor's success.

Marie Antoinette (2006)

Director: Sofia Coppola
Screenwriter: Sofia Coppola
Starring: Kirsten Dunst (Marie Antoinette) and Jason Schwartzman (Louis XVI)

Subject: Queen of France and Navarre Marie Antoinette (Maria Antonia
Josepha Johanna 1755–1793)

Screenwriter and director Sofia Coppola used Antonia Fraser's sympathetic
and well-respected biography *Marie Antoinette: The Journey* (2001) as her
source material. She said, 'I wanted to avoid doing a biopic because I hate
that kind of typical structure … I wanted this to be more impressionistic,
more a portrait of what it might have been like from her point of view'
(quoted in Freer 2006: 150). She continued:

> I feel like everything the public knows about Marie Antoinette is
> based on false information … I was reading Antonia Fraser's book
> and saw there was this real girl – that so much of what we know
> about her is based on propaganda. It was interesting to see the
> other side of what life could have been like for her. I didn't see her
> as a villain. Marie Antoinette was just a teenager when she went to
> Versailles; what she wanted was to stay out late and go to parties.
> The film was about trying to understand her voice and make her
> sympathetic: to see the girl behind all the myths. (Quoted in Woolf
> 2006: 45)

The film covers the period in Antoinette's life from 1768 when, aged 14,
her mother the Empress Maria Theresa of Austria (Marianne Faithfull),
arranges for her marriage to the young dauphin, later Louis XVI (Jason
Schwartzmann), to her arrest and imprisonment in 1792.

The youngest of sixteen children, Antoinette is ignorant of the world
and the expectation of being a married woman. As years pass, and the
French courtiers despise her, the more she gets caught up in a cycle of parties, gambling, shopping and gossip causing fashion magazine *Harper's
Bazaar*'s film critic to note: 'We may be remembered as the *Heat* generation,
but to reduce one of the most fascinating periods in European history to a
tale of shopping and fucking is beyond the pale' (Frostrup 2006: 192).

Neglected by her husband sexually, their relationship deteriorates.
In May 1774 they become King and Queen. Four years, later, there is still
no heir and her brother Joseph (Danny Huston), concerned for his sister's
continued presence in French court life, visits and explains the intricacies
of sexual intercourse and the importance of children to both, and nine

months later, in December 1778, Marie give birth to a daughter. As French financial troubles worsen, their life of extreme luxury and profligacy makes them increasingly unpopular with the people. She has an affair with Count von Fersen (Jamie Dornan) whose look was modelled on Adam Ant (the soundtrack features two of his hits with the band Adam and the Ants). She has further children in 1781, 1785 and 1786 (the last child subsequently dies). As the French Revolution begins to erupt, they become the target of hatred but decide to stay in France, unlike the many nobles who escaped. The last shots of the film are of the palace being stormed and the Royal Family being taken away in June 1792. She would be executed by guillotine in October 1793.

Marie Antoinette was first depicted on film by Anita Louise in *Madame Du Barry* (William Dieterle, 1934) and four years later by Norma Shearer in *Marie Antoinette* (W. S. Van Dyke, 1938). Most recently she was played by Diane Kruger in the French production, *Farewell, My Queen* (Benoît Jacquot, 2012) which offers a fictionalised account of Antoinette's final days, as seen through the eyes of a servant girl.

Despite relying heavily on paintings as visual reference Coppola was keen for her film to be the antithesis of a series of beautifully-lit tableaus in the mode of *Barry Lyndon* (Stanley Kubrick, 1975). She wanted to bring the urgency, decadence and hedonism of the court to life. As she told Matt Woolf, 'filmmakers are the portrait painters of the modern day, bringing to life those realms that are captured for all eternity on canvas' (2006: 45).

A lively and unconventional take on the costume bio-pic, the narrative drive follows a straightforward trajectory but her visual and aural language is anything but expected. There is no attempt by any of the cast to use French or Austrian accents, allowing the cast the freedom to concentrate on their physical and emotional performances. The period covered in the film is from 1768 to 1792, yet there is no attempt to age them, the passing of time instead being shown through the portraits and the number of children depicted in them.

This was a $40 million production, and the filmmakers were given unprecedented access to Versailles. These sequences are filmed as though an episode from MTV's *Welcome to my Crib*. The high-energy score features tracks from 1980s British New Romantic bands Adam and the Ants ('Kings of the Wild Frontier') and Bow Wow Wow ('I Want Candy' and 'Aphrodisiac'). These are interspersed with tender and heart-breaking moments display-

Mary Nighy as Princesse de Lamballe, Kirsten Dunst as Marie Antoinette and Rose Byrne as Duchesse de Polignac in *Marie Antoinette* (2006)

ing the pain, confusion and anguish of this young girl out of her depth, played out against a backdrop of more subdued pieces.

Antoinette is shown as a fragile porcelain doll; when she overhears spiteful gossip about her being barren soon after she becomes an aunt, she rushes to a quiet room, leans against a wall, slides to the ground and sobs. What does a young woman do when so alone? She eats pastries, buys new shoes, hats and clothes – which the film's next energetic montage set to the tune of 'I Want Candy' shows.

A tabloid queen surrounded by gossip, an eighteenth-century style icon with outrageous clothes and hairstyles but her underlying vulnerability is ever-present, and when she is dressed in another ridiculous outfit and overbearing wig, her poses are suffused with the need for acceptance and a look that conveys that age-old question, 'do I look alright in this?' Costume designer Milena Canoero and six assistant designers created the gowns, hats, suits and prop costume pieces. Shoes were designed by Manolo Blahnik and Pompeii, over one hundred wigs and hair pieces were made by Rocchetti & Rocchetti.

The film opens with Antoinette lounging on a *chaise longue* as she eats a beautiful pastry – the room is sumptuous, the soundtrack belts out the punk anthem 'Natural's Not In It' by the Gang of Four. We then rewind back to the fourteen-year-old Marie's entrance into French society as the Austrian princess is sent off to marry the French prince, leaving behind her family, clothes and puppy. It ends with their flight from Versailles to Paris, therefore excluding the dark days leading up to their execution.

Whereas many critics found the juxtaposition of the old and the new unappealing, Pam Cook wrote:

> Coppola's use of travesty in her biopic has contributed to dividing critical opinion. Travesty, a common device in theatre and litera-ture, irreverently wrests its source material from its historical con-text, producing blatantly fake fabrications that challenge accepted notions of authenticity and value. It brazenly mixes high and low culture, and does not disguise its impulse to sweep away tradition. In the case of historical fictions, travesty collapses boundaries of time and place through pastiche, emphasising that history is in the eye of the beholder, whether group or individual. Travesty is play-ful, but it can have a serious purpose: to demonstrate that the past is always viewed through the filter of the present, and represents the vested interests of those who reinvent it. (2006: 36)

Sofia Coppola dismissed criticism that the cast sounded like spoilt 5th Avenue New Yorkers by saying that she wanted 'to emphasise that they are teenagers and to mark the difference between their world and the stuffy court world' (quoted in Freer 2006: 150). This view of Marie Antoinette was shared by historian Simon Schama [in the PBS documentary, *Marie Antoinette,* 2006] in which he described her as a 'Valley Girl' and an 'air-head'. Sam Allis's review of the documentary continued:

> Marie Antoinette was the original Paris Hilton. This hall of fame air-head revelled in a world of endless parties and wore her hair three feet high. This frivolous queen of France was labelled 'Madame Deficit' for her breath-taking spending while the French people starved. If, contrary to common belief, she never said, 'Let them eat cake,' she should have. Historian Simon Schama puts it this way, 'She's got a credit card with no limit really.' (2006)

This is a sympathetic portrait of Marie Antoinette. Perhaps given Coppola's upbringing in a privileged sheltered environment, she felt a kinship with this young woman whose ability to do her job is constantly questioned.

She portrays Antoinette's luxury as little more than a gilded cage. Like all Coppola's films to date, *Marie Antoinette* emphasises the darkness and emptiness that lies beneath a seemingly successful life. Coppola says, 'I think they all [*The Virgin Suicides*, *Lost in Translation* and *Marie Antoinette*] have a similar theme of girls looking for identity and each one takes off where the last one left off. In *Lost in Translation* she's just feeling and searching and in this one there is a complete evolution of a girl finally being a woman (quoted in Freer 2006: 151).

The film opened the 2006 Cannes Film Festival where it was received by a chorus of boos, slow hand claps, catcalls and jeers. Reviews were largely negative, with many criticising its tone and lack of historical integrity. However, despite the anachronisms of the language in the script, the course material of Fraser's biography did ensure that many elements that may have appeared to be fanciful are in fact true. Their marriage was not consummated and Antoinette did receive letters from her mother encouraging her in the bedroom arts. She was also bisexual, and had numerous affairs. The film does perpetuate the myth that she said 'Let them eat cake', which has been discredited.

Jonathan Romney wonders, 'how many critics conflated the two [Marie Antoinette and Sofia Coppola], dismissing the film as really obliquely autobiographical. Some detractors complained that the film wasn't a serious historical drama; others were disappointed it was a more traditional heritage outing than anticipated, rather than the radical genre-busting promise by the chic cast' (2006).

It failed to recoup even half of its $40 million budget at the US box office, taking $15 million domestically. It proved more popular overseas and its final world-wide box office $60 million.

The Queen (2006)

Director: Stephen Frears
Screenwriter: Peter Morgan
Starring: Helen Mirren (Queen Elizabeth II), James Cromwell (Prince Philip), Sylvia Syms (Queen Elizabeth, The Queen Mother) and Michael Sheen (Tony Blair)
Subject: Queen of the United Kingdom and the other Commonwealth realms Elizabeth II (Elizabeth Alexandra Mary, 1926–present)

The Queen was produced by Pathé Pictures and Granada Productions for ITV, opened in the cinemas in September 2006 and was shown on British television on 2 September 2007 to mark the tenth anniversary of Princess Diana's death. It re-united the triptych of director (Stephen Frears), writer (Peter Morgan) and actor (Michael Sheen) that had been behind the Tony Blair/Gordon Brown-themed *The Deal* (Channel 4, 2004). Morgan and Sheen had also collaborated on *The Special Relationship* (2010) about the Blair/Clinton years. Here, their critical gaze turned to the relationship between Queen Elizabeth II, Tony Blair, the British people and the tabloid press for the week-long period in September 1997 following the death of Princess Diana.

Morgan used interviews with 'discreet sources', biographies and news reports to create his screenplay. Neil Tweedie writes, 'Morgan does not claim to have achieved total accuracy in his work. Instead, he seeks 'truthfulness', a plausible version of events that sits comfortably within the characters and the circumstances bequeathed him by real life' (2007). Morgan says, 'You have to ask yourself as a dramatist, do you believe there is a relationship between truth and accuracy? It may not be accurate – you don't know – but is it truthful, is it truthful and fair? Are you giving the character a fair hearing?' (quoted in ibid.)

The film sets up a series of oppositions and explores these through Diana's death and funeral: the forward-thinking Blair government vs old traditions of royalty; public vs private mourning; monarchy vs republic.

Helen Mirren as Queen Elizabeth II and James Cromwell as Prince Philip in *The Queen* (2006)

Helen Mirren as Queen Elizabeth II and James Cromwell as Prince Philip in Despite the film's title, the film is as much about New Labour as it is the Queen: 'Morgan's screenplay provided a more insightful commentary on the instinctively conservative personality of our mysterious, opaque Prime Minister than a hundred political columns' (Billen 2007).

The film's narrative may only take place over one week, but it was one extraordinary week in the life of the Queen. The public and political responses to her were pivotal; this was the first time the Queen had been criticised. It tells an implicit story about the Queen's life and those of her family, courtiers and subjects, and the story as it unfolds says more about the monarchy in the last years of the twentieth century than any multi-part documentary series or birth-to-death bio-pic.

The film is bookended by the Queen and Blair's weekly private audiences. The first, following his election three months before Diana's death, and the last their exchange three months after it, reminiscing on the 'week' that changed them. Blair, still full of the victory after his first six months in the office is very pleased with himself. The Queen swiftly puts him in his place: 'One day they'll turn on you.'

The script is peppered with these knowing asides, ensuring that the film says as much about the dynamics between the monarchy and Parliament of 2006, as it does about 1997: 'It's a portrait of royal power that is as topical as *Desperate Housewives*' (Christopher 2006a). It is the minutiae of the royal daily routine that makes the portrayal of the Queen's life credible, showing her family as one with both a lower- and upper-case F. Bickering, wandering around a cold/damp Balmoral in woolly dressing gowns clutching hot water bottles, her responses to the formal portrait sitting and being woken by the sound of bagpipes all add humanity, which is so appealing. Or the throw-away put-downs, such as when she first meets Tony Blair, bluntly stating: 'You are my tenth Prime minister, Winston Churchill was the first.'

There are the quiet moments that say so much, such as when the Queen reaches out and touch Charles but then holds back, which speaks volumes about their relationship past and present. Yet there are also much more obvious instances of symbolism, for example the parallel between the beautiful majestic stag that the Queen sees whilst out walking and Diana is too clichéd; the Queen begins to weep, grieving for this animal who will be stalked and ultimately killed.

The Queen wishes to remain dignified, always adhering to her mantra of duty first, self second. Charles, recalling Diana who was warm, physical and showed her feelings, believes that they should display some of this emotion publicly. Through persuasion by Blair and the fact that her popularity ratings are at an all-time low, she responds more warmly and slowly the tide of popular opinion turns, culminating in the address to the nation.

Director Stephen Frears has combined these imagined behind-the-scenes moments with real news footage and recreations of key incidents. Sheen's version of Blair's statement on the Sunday morning was word for word, gesture for gesture, pace for pace. Frears described his decision to use archive footage, saying, 'The film hinges on a conflict between one woman who is portrayed by an actress, and another – Diana – who is played by documentary footage. You might think that the pressure was to bring Diana alive, but quite the opposite happened. It would have snapped credibility' (quoted in Christopher 2006a).

After Helen Mirren won the Academy Award for *The Queen*, a palace spokeswoman said, 'I'm sure the Queen will be pleased.' Dalya Alberge reported that, 'the film is regarded as a public relations success for the British monarchy thanks to Mirren's portrayal of the Queen as a resolute sovereign, bound by tradition and protocol, who wrestles with public pressure to shed her veneers of propriety and grieve alongside her nation' (2007). Mirren, in her Academy Award acceptance speech, paid tribute to the woman she portrays, saying, 'I salute her courage and her consistency. And I thank her, because if it wasn't for her, I most certainly would not be here.'

The film's budget was $15 million, and it made $123 million at the worldwide box office. It was to become one of the most critically acclaimed films of 2006 in the US, featuring on many of the critics Top Ten lists. Mirren dominated the major award ceremonies, including an Academy Award and a BAFTA. At the 2014 BAFTA awards she was honoured with its highest award – a Fellowship. It was presented to her by Prince William, the Duke of Cambridge who quipped that she was 'an extremely talented British actress I should probably call Granny'. Mirren would play the Queen, from age 26 to 87 in the Morgan-scripted play *The Audience* (2013). The play recreates a series of weekly meetings the Queen has had with her Prime Ministers from Winston Churchill to David Cameron. The only one not featured was Tony Blair.

Critics rated it highly, with many giving it four or five stars. *Chicago Sun-Times* critic Robert Ebert stated: '*The Queen* could have been told as a scandal sheet story of celebrity gossip. Instead, it becomes the hypnotic tale of two views of the same event – a classic demonstration, in high drama, of how the Establishment has been undermined by publicity. Told in quiet scenes of proper behavior and guarded speech, *The Queen* is a spellbinding story of opposed passions' (2006).

Further viewing

Diana (Olivier Hirschbiegel, 2013); Princess Diana (Naomi Watts)
The Duchess (Saul Dibb, 2008); Georgina Cavendish (Keira Knightley)
The King's Speech (Tom Hooper, 2010); King George VI (Colin Firth)
The Madness of King George (Nicholas Hytner, 1994); King George III (Nigel Hawthorne)
W.E. (Madonna, 2011); Wallis Simpson (Andrea Riseborough), Edward VIII (James D'Arcy)
Young Victoria (Jean-Marc Vallee, 2009); Queen Victoria (Emily Blunt)

EPILOGUE

As I write this in September 2014, there are daily announcements of bio-pics scheduled for release and in the pipeline.

Like all other staple genres, comic book adaptations, thrillers, horrors, rom-coms, the genre will continue to be one that intrigues and fascinates. And as with all other film genres, some will be great successes, and others will fail.

But ultimately biographical-pictures, bio-pics, will succeed if filmmakers find imaginative ways to present the life in question. They will have to manipulate the vast quantities of material available to them, to create a compelling well-constructed narrative. As with documentary films, there will be accusations of bias, what has been included and what has been left out. The interests of the filmmakers will inevitably be reflected in the work. The 'truth' will always be distorted.

'When the legend becomes truth, print the legend.'
– newspaperman Maxwell Scott,
The Man Who Shot Liberty Valance (1962)

BIBLIOGRAPHY

Aitken, Jonathan (2009) 'Nixon v Frost: The true story of what really happened when a British journalist bullied a TV confession out of a disgraced ex-President', *Daily Mail*, 24 January.

Alberge, Dalya (2007) 'Queen Awaits Her Majesty's Pleasure', *The Times*, 27 February.

Alexander, Scott (2002) 'Report on Austin Film Festival 2002'; www.hybridmagazine.com (accessed 10 April 2014).

Allis, Sam (2006) 'Portrait of Queen enlightens and entertains on TV doc *Marie Antoinette*', *Boston Globe*, 25 September.

Andrew, Geoff (6 February 2002) 'Mann Alive', *Time Out*.

Andrew, Geoff (2006a)'*Ed Wood* review', *Time Out*, 26 January.

Andrew, Geoff (2006b)'*American Splendor* review', *Time Out*, 9 February.

Andrews, Nigel (2014) 'Mandela review', *Financial Times*, 2 January.

Anon. (2014) 'The greatest role of all!', *Daily Mail*, 3 January.

Ansen, David (2001) 'Have Yourself a Movie Little Xmas', *Newsweek*, 23 December.

Bayley, John (2002) 'When I Saw *Iris* Again', *The Sunday Telegraph*, 6 January.

Billen, Andrew (2007) 'Tony Blair is like a member of my family', *The Times*, 13 February.

Bingham, Dennis (2010) *Whose Lives Are They Anyway?: The Biopic as Contemporary Film Genre*. New Brunswick, NJ: Rutgers University Press.

Bosley, Rachael K. (2002) 'A Dynamic Portrait', *American Cinematographer*, www.theasc.com/magazine/oct02/frida/index.html (accessed 1 September 2014).

Bracewell, Michael (2002) '*Pollock* review', *Sight and Sound*, June, 47–8.

Bradshaw, Peter (2002) '*Pollock* review', *The Guardian*, 24 May.

____ (2007a) '*Infamous* review', *The Guardian*, 19 January.

____ (2007b) '*Elizabeth: The Golden Age* review', *The Guardian*, 2 November.

____ (2007c) '*I'm Not There* review', *The Guardian*, 21 December.

Brown, Geoff (1998) '*Elizabeth* review', *The Times*, 1 October.

____ (2004) 'Let us now reprise famous men' *The Times, T2*, 23 September.

Byrnes, Paul (2003) '*American Splendor* review', *Sydney Morning Herald*, 11 September.

Caines, Michael (2004) '*Iris* review', *Times Literary Supplement*, 20 February.

Calhoun, Dave (2009) '*Frost/Nixon* review', *Time Out*, 20 January.

Carlin, John (2010) 'Nelson's Victory', *Sunday Times Magazine*, 17 January.

Carnes, Mark C. (ed.) (1996) *Past Imperfect: History According to the Movies*. London: Cassell.

Charity, Tom (1998) 'Virgin records', *Time Out,* 23 September.

Cheng, Scarlet (2001) 'Shhh, Mad Genius at Work', *Los Angeles Times*, 11 February.

Christopher, James (2005) 'The Man Who Broke the Bonk', *The Times*, 3 March.

____ (2006a) 'We are not bemused', *The Times, The Knowledge*, 2 September.

____ (2006b) 'The other Truman show', *The Times*, 19 October.

Clark, John (1994) 'The Wood, The Bad, and the Ugly'. *Premiere*, October, 91–6.

Clarke, Gabriel, McKenna, John and Williams, James (directors) (2009) 'Clough TV Documentary', *ITV Productions*.

Cohen, David (2010) 'Nelson's victory', *Evening Standard*, 14 January.

Colley, Ed (2006) 'The real Truman Show', *Evening Standard*, 19 January.

Cook, Pam (2006) 'Portrait of a Lady: Sofia Coppola', *Sight and Sound*, November, 36–40.

Cooney Carrillo, Jenny (2001), 'Michael Mann and Will Smith On-set Interview', *Total Film*, December, 47.

Cooney, Jenny and Martyn Palmer (2002) 'Will Smith Interview', *Total Film*,

February, 38–42.

Coppola, Don (2002) 'Bringing Historical Characters to Life', *Cineaste*, 27, 2, 16–19.

Crane, Scott (2002) 'Raging Bullshit: *Auto Focus* Is Not My Dads Story', *The Stranger*, 24 October.

Crowther, Bruce (1984) Hollywood Faction: Reality and Myth in the Movies. London: Columbus Books.

Custen, George F. (1992) *Bio/Pics: How Hollywood Constructed Public History*. New Brunswick, NJ: Rutgers University Press.

Dalton, Stephen (2007), 'Subterranean homoerotic blues', *The Times*, 13 December.

Dawson, Jeff (2009), 'The Strife of Brian', *The Sunday Times, Culture Magazine*, 8 March.

DG (2010) *'Invictus* review', *Total Film*, January, 41.

Dickinson, Matt (2009) '*The Damned United*: a big 'ead and shoulders above the opposition', *The Times*, 19 March.

Divine, Christian (2002) 'Peace of Mind: Christian Divine speaks with Akiva Goldsmith', *Creative Screenwriting*, 9, 1, 69–74.

Ebert, Roger (2001) '*Ali* review', *Chicago Sun Times*, 25 December.

____ (2002) '*Auto Focus* review', *Chicago Sun Times*, 25 October.

____ (2004a) '*Ray* review', *Chicago Sun Times*, 28 October.

____ (2004b) '*Beyond the Sea* review', *Chicago Sun Times*, 28 December.

____ (2006) '*The Queen* review', *Chicago Sun Times*, 12 October.

Ellen, Barbara (2002) 'Affliction Empathy', *The Times*, 23 May.

Felperin, Leslie (2005) 'Kinsey review', *Sight and Sound,* March, 55–6.

Ferreyra, Alejandro (2003) 'Chance Encounters: Interview with Michael Gerbois', *Screenwriter*; http://www.angelfire.com/journal2/beemochi/ Gerbosi.htm [(accessed 1 September 2014).

Film4 (2004a) Martin Scorsese on *The Aviator*; www.film4.com http://www. film4.com/special-features/interviews/interview-martin-scorsese-on-the-aviator (accessed 20 April 2014).

____ (2004b) Bill Condon on Kinsey, www.film4.com http://www.film4. com/special-features/interviews/bill-condon-on-kinsey (accessed 7 March 2014).

Fischer, Paul (14 October 2002) 'Interview: Edward Norton', www.darkho-rizons.com.

Freer, Ian (2006) 'Q&A Sofia Coppola', *Empire*, November, 150–1.

French, Philip (2004) 'American Splendor review', The Observer, 4 January.

___ (2013) 'Lincoln review', The Observer, 27 January.

Frostrup, Mariella (2006) 'A fine mess', Harper's Bazaar, October, 192.

Gilbey, Ryan (2014) 'Long Walk to Hollywood: Why has Nelson Mandela been so badly served by cinema?', New Statesman, 7 January.

Gill, Andy (2004)'A Man in Full' Word, December, 58–61.

Goldman, Steve (2002) 'It's a Knockout', Evening Standard, 8 February.

Goodridge, Mike (2004) 'Sex scandal reaps unexpected rewards', Screen International, 22 December.

Griffiths, Ed (2010) 'Sport on the silver screen: was it all part of Mandela's grand design?', The Times, 23 January.

Grundmann, Roy (2005) 'Too Darn Hot: Kinsey & the Culture wars', Cineaste, 30, 2, 4–11.

Hamilos, Paul (2005) 'Charles and I', The Guardian, 6 June.

Hardie, Giles (2013) 'Big names, big flops: Why the biopics have failed in 2013', Sydney Morning Herald, 25 October.

Hastings, Chris (2005) 'The stuff of magic', The Sunday Telegraph, 19 June.

Hazelton, John (2005) 'Life Lessons: marketing Biopics', Screen International, 18 November.

Hensher, Philip (2005) 'Gay for Today', The Guardian, 24 November.

Hislop, Ian (tx 9 April 2014) 'Ian Hislop's Olden Days: episode 1', BBC TV.

Hoggard, Liz (2006) 'Interview with Daniel Craig', The Observer, 31 December.

Holzer, Harold (2012) 'What's True and False in Lincoln Movie', The Daily Beast, 22 November.

Hornaday, Ann (2002) 'Iris: A Love Story In Glorious Full Bloom', Washington Post, 15 February.

Hoyle, Ben (2008) 'Nixon film may be a thinking man's Rocky – but I was not the underdog', The Times, 15 October.

Ide, Wendy (2007)'Hard to be a Woman', The Times, The Knowledge, 31 March.

Kauffmann, Stanley (2002) 'A Couple of Genuises', The New Republic; http://www.newrepublic.com/article/couple-genuises (accessed 1 September 2014)

Kleinman, Geoffrey (2003) Interview with Ed Harris, 28 February; www.

dvdtalk.com (accessed 28 November 2013).

Landy, Marcia ed. (2000) The Historical Film: History and Memory in Media. New Brunswick, New Jersey: Rutgers University Press.

Levy, Shawn (2005) 'The Man Who Would Be Capote', *Portland Oregonion*, 20 October.

Litt, Toby (13 December 2007) 'Star gazing', *The New Statesman*.

Lloyd, Rebecca (2011) 'The rise of the political biopic', *The New Statesman*, 15 December.

MacDonald Fraser, George (1996) revised and updated The Hollywood History of the World. London: Harvill Press [First published 1988 Michael Joseph]

Mackaman, Tom (3 April 2013) 'Understanding Lincoln: An interview with historian Allen Guelzo'. *World Socialist website*, www.wsws.org

Maconie, Stuart (2005) 'Flying by the Seat of Her Pants', *Word*, August, 114–15.

Marriott, Edward (1998) 'Why Elizabeth Rules America', *Evening Standard*, 17 December.

Matheou, Demetrios (2002) 'Painting the big picture', *The Sunday Telegraph*, 28 April.

McDougal, Dennis (2004)'Kevin Spacey's Battle for Bobby Darin', *The New York Times*, 21 November.

McIlvanney, Hugh (29 March 2009), 'The Voice of Sport: Case of Write and Wrong', *The Sunday Times*.

McLean, Craig (2007) 'Samantha Morton: Why does our boldest film actress feel so persecuted for her loyalty to British indie cinema?', *The Independent*, 2 April.

Miller, Robert Milton (1983) Star Myths: Show-Business Biographies on Film. Metuchen, NJ & London: The Scarecrow Press, Inc.

Mitchell, Elvis (2001) 'Master of the Boast, King of the Ring, Vision of the Future', *The New York Times*, 25 December.

Morgenstern, Joe (2003) 'Costner Rides Again: *Open Range* Speaks Softly, Packs Western Wallop', *Wall Street Journal*, 8 August.

Murray, Rebecca (2004) 'Kevin Spacey Brings His Labor of Love to the Screen: Spacey on Bobby Darin and *Beyond the Sea*' www.moviesabout.com (accessed 12 January 2014).

Nathan, Ian (2009) '*Frost/Nixon review*', *Empire*, January, 62–3.

NB (2011) 'How to make a good biopic', *The Economist*, 29 November.

Nicholson, William (2007) 'William the Queen maker', *The Times*, 27 October.

Nisbet, Matthew C. (2010) 'Reconsidering the Image of Scientists in Film and Television', 5 May www.scienceblogs.com (accessed 23 March 2014).

Owen, Richard (2007) 'Rome condemns Elizabeth again – this time over film of her reign', *The Times*, 11 July.

Palmer, Martyn (2002) 'The Outsider', *Total Film*, March, 46–50.

Perlstein, Rick (2009) 'Flirtation, seduction, betrayal ... it's all there: Historians, politicians and broadcasters give us their expert opinions on *Frost/Nixon*', *The Observer*, 18 January; http://www.theguardian.com/film/2009/jan/18/frost-nixon-review (accessed 1 September 2014).

Pulver, Andrew (2003) '*Frida* review', *The Guardian*, 28 February.

Quinn, Anthony (2007) '*Elizabeth: The Golden Age* review', *The Independent*, 2 November.

_____ (2007b) '*I'm Not There* review', *The Independent*, 21 December.

Robey, Tim (2003) 'Down the drain of depravity', *The Telegraph*, 7 March.

Robson, Leo (27 March 2009) 'We're not famous anymore', *Times Literary Supplement*.

Rockwell, Cynthia (2002) '*A Beautiful Mind*', *Cineaste*, 27, 3, 36–7.

Romney, Jonathan (2006), 'Care for ein Kirstendunst?' *Independent on Sunday*, 22 October.

Rooney, David (1998)'*Elizabeth* review', *Variety*, 9 September.

Ryfle, Steve (2005) 'Writers Beware! Column', *Creative Screenwriting*, September/October, 46–7.

Salisbury, Bill (1994) 'King of the Offbeat'. *Fangoria*, 138, 66–70.

Scott, A. O. (2006) 'Truman Capote's Journey on 'In Cold Blood, Again', *The New York Times*, 13 October.

Shoard, Catherine (2005), '*Ray* review', *Sunday Telegraph*, 23 January.

Shone, Tom (2013) 'I had to change: The Stephen Spielberg interview' *The Sunday Times, Culture Magazine*, 20 January, 4–5.

Silberg, Jon (2007) 'Deconstructing Bob Dylan', *American Cinematographer*; https://www.theasc.com/ac_magazine/November2007/ImNotThere/page1.php (accessed 1 September 2014).

Singh, Anita (2009) 'Martin Scorsese's portrayal of Frank Sinatra angers family', *The Telegraph*, 18 August.

Smith, Adam (2014) 'Tribute: Philip Seymour Hoffman 1967–2014', *Empire*, April, 26–7.

Sneider, Jeff (26 December 2013) 'Megan Good's One Wish for Christmas: To play Whitney Houston in Biopic', *The Wrap*

Sorlin, Pierre (1980) The Film in History: Restaging the Past. Oxford: Basil Blackwell

Stone, Mary (2013) 'Interview on Talking History, News Talk Radio', 14 October; www.savehitchcock.com (accessed 1 April 2014).

Teeman, Tim (2009) 'The Conversation: Peter Morgan', *The Times*, 21 March.

Thomson, Desson (2004)'Spacey's Shallow Sea', *Washington Post*, 31 December.

Tobias, Scott (2003) '*American Splendor* review', *AV Club*; http://www.avclub.com/review/american-splendor-5499 (accessed 1 September 2014).

Tucker, Nicky (2001) *Iris* Programme Notes, Curzon Cinema.

Tuckman, Jo (2001) 'That Frida feeling', *The Guardian*, 30 August.

Tweedie, Neil (2007) 'How they created the Queen for the screen', *The Telegraph*, 27 February.

Walker, Alexander (2002), '*Frida* review', *Evening Standard*, 3 September.

Warren, Bill (1994) 'Ed Wood for better or worse', *Fangoria*, 137, 34–8.

Weinstein Company, The (2007) 'I'm, Not There Production Notes', www.twcpublicity.com/download/production/productionnotes.doc [accessed 3 February 2014]

Williams, Linda Ruth (2003) 'Swing high, swing low: *Auto Focus* review', *Sight and Sound*, March, 36.

Williams, Sally (2013) 'The making of *Mandela: Long Walk to Freedom*', *The Telegraph*, 7 December.

Woolf, Matt (2006) 'Don't Mention the Cake', *Royal Academy Magazine*, Winter, 45.

INDEX